Advance praise for
Leading the Malcolm Baldrige Way

We Baldrige aficionados love to brag that the Baldrige Criteria is non-prescriptive. Unfortunately, this leaves a new leader at a loss for a source of the "answers." This book is a source of the answers assembled by two of the foremost Baldrige consultants culled from many Baldrige leaders and from working with and for an extensive list of high-performing organizations. The information is provided through quotes and anecdotes that provide convincing evidence, key learnings, and insights. I wish that I had this book available to me when I started our Baldrige journey!

E. David Spong
Retired leader of Boeing Mobility—formerly Airlift & Tanker
(Baldrige Award recipient in 1998) and Boeing Support Systems—
formerly Aerospace Support (Baldrige Award recipient in 2003)

How much better of a "game plan" can you have than what Glenn and Kay have put together in this book? That is, if you want to take your company to world class status. Winners are willing to do the things that others aren't. It's that simple. A great read for any executive.

Jordan Case
President of Park Place Lexus (Baldrige Award recipient in 2005)

It took Elevations Credit Union 55 years to generate $63 million in capital. In April 2009 we began deploying the concepts outlined in this book. Five years later when we received the Malcolm Baldrige National Quality Award, we had doubled our capital while reducing the overall risk of the Credit Union . . . during the Great Recession. Read more about our journey in this book.

Gerry Agnes
President and CEO of Elevations Credit Union
(Baldrige Award recipient in 2014)

Transforming organizations to make them more agile, efficient and market-focused has become a competitive imperative. Using the proven Baldridge framework and relying on deep expertise to generate sustainable results and competitive advantage, the authors provide an indispensable perspective and valuable advice towards achieving a quality transformation. Whether you are seeking incremental improvement to your business or are ready to undertake the quality journey associated with achieving the Baldrige Award, this is an indispensable field guide.

Scott McIntyre
Managing Partner, PricewaterhouseCoopers Public Sector Practice

Kay and Glenn have combined their decades of experience to research and highlight world-class examples of employee engagement, and why it matters. A must-read for any organizational leader.

Al Faber
President and CEO, Baldrige Foundation

The life we live is guided by the books we read. The bible guides many of us on how best to live our lives. The Baldrige principles and this book really shape how we lead our organizations and how we create the best possible outcomes for the people in them.

Tommy Gonzalez
City Manager of the City of El Paso and former City Manager
of the City of Irving (Baldrige Award recipient in 2012)

As a leader whose leadership has been transformed using the Baldrige Criteria for Performance Excellence, I greatly recommend this book. I know firsthand that using the Baldrige Criteria has helped my organization attain improved alignment and exceptional results. Read this book if you desire a systematic way to improve. Your leadership will be positively impacted!

Dr. JoAnn Sternke
Superintendent, Pewaukee School District
(Baldrige Award recipient in 2013)

The authors did a great job highlighting many Baldrige winning organizations across various industries—giving readers different perspectives and scenarios to apply the information. The objectives and checklists that bookend each chapter really give the readers a solid set up and time for reflection. The book is organized, clear to follow, and easy to navigate. I recommend this book to any person who is interested in continual improvement, winning results, and achieving ever increasing levels of operational excellence.

Ken Schiller
Co-owner and Cofounder of K&N Management
(Baldrige Award recipient in 2010)

This book is the perfect tool for any leader interested in unlocking their team's potential through an energized and connected workforce. Kay and Glenn have done a great job in describing pathways which address a wide variety of the situations every leader will experience throughout a career. I wish it had been on my bookshelf for the last 30 years!

Stan Waterhouse
President and Chief Executive Officer,
Senior Quality Lifestyles Corporation

Among its other strengths, this book illustrates how the Baldrige approach is highly complementary and supportive of the Lean methodology, both as a detailed improvement system and high-level culture. Engaging employees has long been understood to be a way of improving quality, delighting customers, creating a better workplace, and succeeding as an organization over the long term. This book is full of stories that will inspire you in your journey toward a Baldrige Award or, more importantly, meaningful continuous improvement and sustained success.

Mark Graban
Author of *Lean Hospitals* and coauthor of *Healthcare Kaizen*

LEADING THE
MALCOLM
BALDRIGE
WAY

KAY KENDALL
GLENN BODINSON, FACHE

New York   Chicago   San Francisco   Athens   London   Madrid
Mexico City   Milan   New Delhi   Singapore   Sydney   Toronto

1 2 3 4 5 6 7 8 9   LCR   21 20 19 18 17 16

ISBN   978-1-259-58866-2
MHID   1-259-58866-1

e-ISBN   978-1-259-58867-9
e-MHID   1-259-58867-X

This publication is designed to provide accurate and authoritative information in regard to the subject matter covered. It is sold with the understanding that neither the author nor the publisher is engaged in rendering legal, accounting, securities trading, or other professional services. If legal advice or other expert assistance is required, the services of a competent professional person should be sought.
    —*From a Declaration of Principles Jointly Adopted by a Committee of the American Bar Association and a Committee of Publishers and Associations*

Library of Congress Cataloging-in-Publication Data

Names: Kendall, Kay, author. | Bodinson, Glenn, author.
Title: Leading the Malcolm Baldrige way : how world-class leaders align their
    organizations to deliver exceptional results / Kay Kendall and Glenn Bodinson.
Description: New York : McGraw-Hill, [2017] | Includes bibliographical references.
Identifiers: LCCN 2016028725 (print) | LCCN 2016042770 (ebook) | ISBN
    9781259588662 (alk. paper) | ISBN 1259588661 | ISBN 9781259588679 () |
    ISBN 125958867X
Subjects: LCSH: Malcolm Baldrige National Quality Award. | Total quality
    management. | Leadership. | Organizational effectiveness. | Corporate culture.
    | Baldrige, Malcolm, 1922-1987.
Classification: LCC HD62.15 .K457 2017 (print) | LCC HD62.15 (ebook) | DDC
    658.4/013--dc23
LC record available at https://na01.safelinks.protection.outlook.com/?url=https
    %3a%2f%2flccn.loc.gov%2f2016028725&data=01%7c01%7ckari.black
    %40mheducation.com%7c59d90d74141942ab770e08d3de6a8aa9%7cf919
    b1efc0c347358fca0928ec39d8d5%7c1&sdata=y539lDYZrvrOfnJcKJazR8
    muZ8bxT6WOJf5Bum9hko0%3d

Contents

Acknowledgments

First, we'd like to thank the Baldrige Program for Performance Excellence, a team of tireless staff members who manage the program, provide a wealth of educational materials, administer the award program, and lead a volunteer workforce of examiners and judges. A special thank you goes to Dr. Curt Reimann, the program's first Director, and Dr. Harry Hertz, Director Emeritus, for spending the time with us to share their insights on the very beginning of the program and its evolution over the years. Our time in service to the program as examiners has been the best professional development we could have ever asked for and has given us the added bonus of a large network of equally committed people who are passionate about helping organizations improve to strengthen American competitiveness.

We also thank those leaders of Baldrige Award recipient organizations who made themselves available—some on multiple occasions—to tell their stories and share their wisdom: Gerry Agnes, Dr. Joe Alexander, Jim Berry, Joan Brennan, Joe Brescia, Diane Brockmeier, Allison Carter, Jordan Case, Dr. Glenn Crotty, Dale Crownover, Jake Dablemont, Rob Ecklin, Matt Flemming, Stan Frink, Tommy Gonzalez, Dr. Katherine Gottlieb, Brenda Grant, Dr. Bruce Kintz, Michael Levinson, Terry May, Scott McIntyre, Lynn Nelson, Jayne Pope, Larry Potterfield, David Ramsey, Peter Raymond, Rick Rodman, Sr. Mary Jean Ryan, Dr. Mike Sather, Ken Schiller, Ken Schnitzer, Dr. David Spong, Dr. Rulon Stacy, Dr. JoAnn Sternke,

Quint Studer, David Tilton, Paul Worstall, Allyson Young, and Harry Zechman.

Others from their organizations who helped pull the content for the figures: Jamie Capehart at Park Place Lexus, Deanna Herwald at MidAmericaUSA, Katie Weathers at Elevations Credit Union, Lynn Nelson at North Mississippi Health Services Center, Priscilla Nuwash at Poudre Valley Health System, and Susan Muener at Pewaukee School District.

We must extend a special thanks to Larry Potterfield, founder and CEO of MidwayUSA, who invited us up to spend a day there because "45 minutes on the phone wasn't going to be enough time" to tell their story. Wow, were they right. They are, as they claim, the purest Baldrige colony on the planet. They use the Baldrige Framework to run their business. It shows in their culture, processes, and results. It is the only organization that we have visited that doesn't have to prepare for a Baldrige Award site visit. They live it every day. And they proved that when they won their second Baldrige Award in 2015.

We also interviewed the leaders of organizations that are recipients of Baldrige-based award programs: Maryruth Butler, Maureen Carland, Brian Dieter, Deb Fournier, Melissa Graham, Marcia Jackson, Dr. Steve Mansfield, Karen Kiel Rosser, and Pam Stoyanoff.

We are fortunate to have on our team an exceptionally talented graphic artist, Adina Sapronetti, who created the figures for the book and who creates amazing figures to help some of our clients better tell their stories in their award applications.

From McGraw-Hill Education, we would like to thank our Executive Editor, Donya Dickerson for contacting us with the concept for the book and shepherding it (and us!) through its publication.

We are extremely grateful to our clients, many of whom are featured in this book. As much as we have coached you,

you have taught us. You've given us a firsthand look at the many ways that employee engagement manifests itself in organizations and the privilege of experiencing that "palpable" culture of excellence.

Finally, thank you to our families and friends who put up with us during this process when it seemed as though we had no other topic of conversation than this book.

Foreword

I've been a health care executive for 30 years. Early in my career, I was fortunate to work in SSM Healthcare where I watched Sister Mary Jean Ryan adopt the Baldrige Criteria and lead the process. I was so captivated by the journey and the ability I saw to align an entire organization toward one common goal that I began then and there the process to learn and adopt the Criteria.

Soon thereafter, I accepted the position of President and Chief Executive Officer at Poudre Valley Health System, and I immediately knew that I was going to use the Baldrige Criteria as the framework for how we elevated the performance of the organization from good to world-class. In health care, being good is not sufficient. We need to be at the top of our game every day, and using the Baldrige Criteria is the best way that I know to ensure that.

One of the most powerful aspects of using the Baldrige Criteria is its ability to help leaders align and engage their workforce in the vision, mission, and values of the organization to accomplish the most important objectives. In this authoritative book by Kay and Glenn, you'll see how many organizations have done just that—organizations in the health care, education, manufacturing, service, small businesses, government, and not-for-profit sectors. They range from the very small, some in challenging remote locations, to the very large with multiple locations across the country.

This book is the result of Kay and Glenn interviewing more than 50 CEOs and other senior leaders of Baldrige Award-winning organizations and other Baldrige-based programs. Through these interviews, you'll learn how these leaders transformed their organizations as they share their lessons learned. These lessons are presented in a compelling manner and reinforced with insightful questions at the end of the chapters.

Leading the Malcolm Baldrige Way addresses several questions that most leaders have at the crossroads of embarking on a large-scale change initiative. I wish this book had been available when my organization embarked on our journey to performance excellence.

As the current Chair of the Baldrige Board of Overseers, I know the power of the Baldrige Criteria to help American organizations compete against global competition to ensure that jobs are retained and created to support a strong economy and opportunities for employment. No matter where your organization is on your journey to achieving improved results in a challenging environment, this book can help you take it to the next level.

Rulon F. Stacey, PhD, FACHE
Navigant Consulting
Chair, Board of Overseers, Malcolm Baldrige National Quality Award
Past Chair, ACHE Board of Governors
Former CEO, Poudre Valley Health System, a 2008 Baldrige Award recipient

An Introduction to Baldrige

- How did the Malcolm Baldrige National Quality Award begin?
- Who was Malcolm Baldrige?
- How was the Malcolm Baldrige National Quality Program developed?
- How has the Malcolm Baldrige National Quality Program changed over time?
- How has the reach of the Malcolm Baldrige National Quality Program expanded?
- What impact has the Malcolm Baldrige National Quality Program had?
- What are the elements of the Baldrige Excellence Framework?

A ll of the organizations featured in this book have in common their use of the Malcolm Baldrige Excellence Framework.* All of the leaders we interviewed professed a strong conviction that the Baldrige framework enabled their organizations to be successful, even in difficult circumstances of an economic downturn, increasing competition, and other challenges.

While the organizations have their use of Baldrige in common, it is fascinating to observe their differences. Dr. JoAnn Sternke, superintendent of the Pewaukee School

---

* Brief descriptions of all of the organizations featured in this book can be found in Appendix D.

District (a Baldrige Award recipient in 2013) gets excited about the relevance of the framework across organizations. "What is so impressive about the Baldrige Criteria is that they apply to any organization, in any sector, of any size." Diane Brockmeier, CEO of Mid-America Transplant Services (a 2015 Baldrige Award recipient) said that when she attended the Baldrige Quest for Excellence® conference in 2006, she followed the track of presentations by Park Place Lexus (a 2005 Baldrige Award recipient). "The idea that we could get so much learning from a car dealership was amazing. Their world is so different from ours in organ donation and transplants, but the common use of the Baldrige Criteria provided that transferability of best practices and lessons learned."

Before we understand how to use the Baldrige Criteria, it's important to understand how the Criteria first came into being.

How Did the Malcolm Baldrige National Quality Award Begin?

In the mid-1980s, American industry had become increasingly uncompetitive against foreign manufacturers who understood the need for and had the ability to deliver high-quality products. The Secretary of Commerce at the time, Malcolm Baldrige, had spent a long, successful career in industry prior to his appointment as secretary under President Ronald Reagan. He believed that a renewed focus on quality and the principles of quality management were critical to the United States' ability to compete successfully in an increasingly crowded marketplace. He also believed that the manufacturing sector, in particular, was vital to maintaining jobs and improving the nation's productivity. He helped draft one of the early versions of the legislation that ultimately became the foundation for the award that bears his name.

A National Productivity Advisory Committee, chaired by Jack Grayson, led the effort to develop a proposal for a public law that would create a national quality award with multiple purposes:

- Helping to stimulate American companies to improve quality and productivity for the pride of recognition while obtaining a competitive edge through increased profits;
- Recognizing the achievements of those companies that improve the quality of their goods and services and providing an example to others;
- Establishing guidelines and criteria that can be used by business, industrial, governmental, and other organizations in evaluating their own quality improvement efforts; and
- Providing specific guidance for other American organizations that wish to learn how to manage for high quality by making available detailed information on how winning organizations were able to change their cultures and achieve eminence.[1]

The Malcolm Baldrige National Quality Improvement Act of 1987 (Public Law 100-107) was signed into law on August 20, 1987, and approved by President Ronald Reagan. Its original scope was for organizations in the manufacturing, service, and small business sectors. The scope was expanded in 1999 to include health care and education organizations and again in 2005 to include nonprofit and government organizations.

Who Was Malcolm Baldrige?

Malcolm Baldrige Jr. was the son of a congressman from Nebraska. He had a long career culminating in his role as chairman and CEO of Scovill, Inc. before being nominated to be the Secretary of Commerce by President Ronald Reagan on December 11, 1980, and confirmed by the United States Senate on January 22, 1981.

In addition to his managerial expertise, Malcolm Baldrige was an avid horseman and won several awards as a professional team roper on the rodeo circuit. He was the Professional Rodeo Man of the Year in 1980 and was elected, posthumously, to the National Cowboy Hall of Fame in 1999. Tragically, Malcolm Baldrige died on July 25, 1987, as the result of injuries he sustained in an accident from a calf-roping competition in a rodeo event.

Because of his perseverance in promoting quality management on behalf of American competitiveness, Congress elected to name the new quality award in his honor.

Also perhaps of interest, his sister, Letitia Baldrige, was an etiquette expert and public relations executive who served as Jacqueline Kennedy's social secretary. She was a stalwart supporter of the Baldrige Program and attended many award ceremonies as well as many of the examiner recognition events during which she expressed her deep appreciation for all of the volunteer time these examiners donate on behalf of the Malcolm Baldrige National Quality Award and their nation.

How Was the Malcolm Baldrige National Quality Program Developed?

The "home" for the award program had already been determined to be under the auspices of the Department of Commerce, specifically with the National Bureau of Standards (NBS), which later became the National Institute of Standards and Technology (NIST). The National Bureau of Standards had an excellent reputation as an apolitical agency with credibility for working with industry. Another reason this home was a good fit was the prevalence of chemists for whom analysis and systems thinking are second nature. Both of these components are integral with the Baldrige framework and the assessment process.

Dr. Curt Reimann, then deputy director of the NBS National Measurement Laboratory, was asked to lead the effort to create the program supporting the new presidential award. The legislation did not specify the elements to implement the program: the Criteria, the assessment process, the judging process, or even the funding. There was initially no government funding, so a private-sector foundation had to be established. Examiners and judges—all volunteers—had to be recruited and trained. All of this effort was expected to be completed so that the first Malcolm Baldrige National Quality Awards could be given in November 1988, before President Reagan's term of office ended.

Incredibly, Dr. Reimann and a very small staff were able to enlist the volunteer help of numerous quality experts and business executives across all sectors—even those sectors not yet eligible to apply for the award—to review and provide feedback on the criteria for the award. Recruitment of and training for 102 examiners and 21 senior examiners was completed to meet the aggressive schedule. Dr. Reimann also recruited a nine-member panel of judges who represented a balance across the manufacturing and service sectors as well as acknowledged quality experts such as Blanton Godfrey, formerly of the Juran Institute, Inc. A board of overseers was established, and the Foundation for the Malcolm Baldrige National Quality Award was made official through a signed agreement with the Department of Commerce and became a 501(c)(3) charitable nonprofit corporation.

"This was the most energizing period of my life. Entirely unique. Anyone you called for help gave you the names of another six people to reach out to. And they'd give you another six," says Dr. Reimann. "You'd call a meeting, and people would cancel what they were doing and show up."

On March 31, 1988, the Baldrige Program was officially launched by President Reagan at a White House ceremony. This highly publicized event invited companies to use this new standard (the Award Criteria) to compare their progress against the country's very best organizations. Later that same year, on November 14, also at the White House, President Reagan personally congratulated the first Baldrige Award recipients: Globe Specialty Metals, Inc. (formerly Globe Metallurgical Inc.), Motorola, Inc., and Westinghouse Electric Corporation Commercial Nuclear Fuel Division.

How Has the Malcolm Baldrige National Quality Program Changed over Time?

As mentioned previously in this chapter, additional sectors were added to those originally eligible to apply for the award. The Criteria have been reviewed and revised multiple times, with input sought from thought leaders, academics, business executives, applicants, and examiners. It currently is refreshed every two years. When the Criteria first were published, there were 42 items. Over time, this number has been reduced to 17. A Glossary was added in 1996, growing from a mere nine entries to over seven pages of well-crafted, insightful definitions.

The Organizational Profile was added in 2001. The questions in the Organizational Profile provoke dialogue among senior leaders to be clear they are on the same page. It takes a tacit agreement on what is most important to the organization and makes it explicit. Dale Crownover, CEO of Texas Nameplate Company, Inc. (a Baldrige Award small business recipient in 1998 and 2004), says, "I love the Organizational Profile. They didn't have that when we first started using the Baldrige Criteria. If anyone asked me how to get started now,

I would say the Organizational Profile is the first thing I'd have folks work on." Alignment and focus in the application and in the organization itself all begin with the answers to the questions in the Organizational Profile.

Dr. JoAnn Sternke, superintendent of the Pewaukee School District (a Baldrige Award recipient in 2013) shares Dale's view. "The Organizational Profile—those questions are golden. Getting your senior leaders to identify the strategic challenges and the strategic advantages for your organization is huge. And they change over time, so you have to keep having the conversation."

Dr. Glenn Crotty, COO of the Charleston Area Medical Center (a Baldrige Award recipient in 2015), said, "One of the things that we did as we matured along the journey was to go back to the Organizational Profile. We understood the questions better, and we understood now the importance of aligning the questions about the requirements of the customers and stakeholders with the key requirements of the processes. We then were able to engage those customers and stakeholders differently."

One of the most significant changes was the intentional renaming of the "Award Criteria" to the "Criteria for Performance Excellence" in 1997. This was more than a symbolic gesture. It was an acknowledgment that many, many organizations were using the Criteria to assess against a standard of excellence without any intent of applying for an award. Cargill Industries and the Eaton Corporation have openly described their internal assessment programs using the Baldrige Criteria and its value in driving improvement in the business units that embrace it. The name change also reinforced the original purpose of the Criteria, which was to help organizations achieve performance excellence. The award merely served as encouragement for organizations to begin the pursuit and as recognition for the achievement of performance excellence.

Concepts have been added to the Criteria as they became increasingly relevant in the environment in which organizations were operating. This is determined by monitoring industry and academic literature and by observing trends in high-performing organizations. For example, public responsibility and corporate citizenship were added in 1993. Dr. Harry Hertz, Director Emeritus of the program, described some of the changes to Item 1.1, Senior Leadership. "We've seen changes in the role of senior leaders. For example, their personal role in leadership development and succession planning was the result of Jack Welch's demonstrable commitment to both through GE's learning center in Crotonville." An increased emphasis on governance and ethics showed up in 2003 following the Enron and Tyco scandals. Strategic challenges, strategic advantages, and core competencies were added in 2007.

Also in 2007, the explicit concept of employee engagement first appeared. Harry explained, "What we were seeing with both employees and customers was that satisfaction didn't drive loyalty. We also reviewed research that showed a direct relationship between engaged employees and customer loyalty. We saw employee engagement becoming an increasing hallmark of Baldrige Award recipients." Innovation with intelligent risk taking and the identification of strategic opportunities, along with the use of social media, were concepts introduced in 2013. In the 2015–2016 Baldrige Excellence Framework, three new concepts were added: change management, big data, and climate change.

As stated in the release of the 2015–2016 Baldrige Excellence Framework, "with every revision of the Criteria, there is one overarching purpose: that the Criteria always reflect the leading edge of validated leadership and performance practice."[2]

How Has the Reach of the Malcolm Baldrige National Quality Program Expanded?

Most states or regions have a Baldrige-based program, as do some sectors such as the AHCA/NCAL (American Health Care Association/National Center for Assisted Living) National Quality Award for long-term care and assisted living, and the National Housing Quality Award (NHQA). In 2005, Baldrige-based state, local, and sector programs created the Alliance for Performance Excellence to coordinate resources and expenses. These programs serve as a "feeder" system for applicants and examiners to the national program but also serve as more approachable, less intimidating avenues for organizations to begin their journeys. Many of the organizations featured in this book started their journeys with their state program. You can read more about this approach in Chapter 14.

Of the approximately 100 performance or business excellence programs around the world, most use the Baldrige Criteria or criteria similar to Baldrige as their models for performance excellence.

What Impact Has the Malcolm Baldrige National Quality Program Had?

The ratio of the Baldrige Program's benefits to the U.S. economy to its costs is estimated at 820 to 1.[3] The award applicants from 2010 to 2014 represent 537,871 jobs across 2,520 work sites, with over $80 billion in revenue/budgets and approximately 436 million customers served.

The 109 unique award recipients (including seven two-time award recipients) serve as national role models and share best practices with other organizations. There have been 1,613 award applications submitted over the life of the program, and more than 11,100 examiners have been trained at the national level. The extent of their voluntary contri-butions cannot be overstated. For example, in 2015, 349 Baldrige examiners volunteered roughly $5.3 million in their services. In the same year, state Baldrige-based examiners volunteered approximately $30 million in services.

> "I honestly in my heart believe that because we participated in the Baldrige program and because it gave us that consistent feedback, there are people who are alive today who wouldn't have been had we not been so committed to the Baldrige process."
>
> —**Dr. Rulon Stacey,** former CEO, Poudre Valley Health System, 2008 Baldrige Award recipient

Several recent studies about the use of the Baldrige Cri-teria in health care organizations show that Baldrige Award recipients:

- Are superior to national averages on all but one of five mortality measures
- Perform 13 percent better than the national average, demonstrate central line infection rates that are more than 40 percent better, and demonstrate colon surgery infection rates that are almost 50 percent better
- Perform significantly better on most of the Centers for Medicare and Medicaid Services measures than the national average
- Perform better than the national averages on hospital readmissions
- Excel on five of six infection measures
- Demonstrate patient safety results and pneumonia immunization rates that are significantly better than the national average

- Excel on patient satisfaction, being clearly superior on two important summary measures: "highly satisfied" and "would recommend"[4]

Another study in the manufacturing sector found that each of the Baldrige Award recipients in that sector experienced remarkable financial growth in the few years leading up to the subsequent award and in the years after winning the award.[5]

What Are the Elements of the Baldrige Excellence Framework?

The three elements are:

- The Criteria for Performance Excellence (the Organizational Profile, six Process categories, and one Results category)
- Core values and concepts
- Guidelines for responding to the Criteria and evaluating and scoring processes and results

Tommy Gonzalez, former city manager of the City of Irving (a Baldrige Award government recipient in 2012), says, "Unless you see the Criteria and how they're all [all of the elements] intertwined, you don't get their power." Pam Stoyanoff, COO of Methodist Health System (a 2015 recipient of the Texas Award for Performance Excellence), described how writing the application against the Criteria helped her organization. "We were more disjointed than I realized. We do lots of good things, but they weren't tied together. For instance, it opened our eyes to the fact that we were missing opportunities by not aggregating and trending patient complaints across the system. We learned that many of our processes were more implicit and less explicit. The Criteria made us see that."

FIGURE 1.1 The Baldrige Excellence Framework

Dr. Steve Mansfield, CEO of Methodist Health System, said that using the Baldrige framework caused helpful reflection for him as a leader. "Rethinking the way you do your work purposefully, with structure, is a valuable tool for driving consistency. There are a lot of advantages to having one playbook for the way you lead the organization."

In addition, Notes and a Glossary provide other helpful information. The Baldrige Excellence Framework (Figure 1.1) is available in three versions: one for manufacturing, service, small business, and nonprofit organizations; a second for education organizations; and a third for health care organizations.

What you'll notice in the overview of the 2015–2016 Baldrige Criteria in Table 1.1 is that nearly half, 45 percent to be precise, of the total possible points are assigned to Results. Anyone who still believes this is just a "quality" award hasn't looked at the Criteria in years. Something else to be noted is

TABLE 1.1 2015–2016 Baldrige Criteria Overview:
Categories, Items, and Point Values

CATEGORY	ITEMS	POINT VALUES	
1 Leadership			120
	1.1 Senior Leadership	70	
	1.2 Governance and Societal Responsibility	50	
2 Strategy			85
	2.1 Strategy Development	45	
	2.2 Strategy Implementation	40	
3 Customers			85
	3.1 Voice of the Customer	40	
	3.2 Customer Engagement	45	
4 Measurement, Analysis, and Knowledge Management			90
	4.1 Measurement, Analysis, and Improvement of Organizational Performance	45	
	4.2 Knowledge Management, Information, and Information Technology	45	
5 Workforce			85
	5.1 Workforce Environment	40	
	5.2 Workforce Engagement	45	
6 Operations			85
	6.1 Work Processes	45	
	6.2 Operational Effectiveness	40	
7 Results			450
	7.1 Product and Process Results	120	
	7.2 Customer-Focused Results	80	
	7.3 Workforce-Focused Results	80	
	7.4 Leadership and Governance Results	80	
	7.5 Financial and Market Results	90	
Total Points			1000

that the Leadership category, Category 1, is weighted more heavily than the other Process categories. This is because of the overwhelming evidence of the importance of leadership in world-class organizations. And as the business world has become more unpredictable with competition emerging from unimagined sources, leadership becomes even more important to ensure an organization that is successful now and in the future.

Two other adjectives are often used to describe the Criteria: holistic and nonprescriptive. Holistic refers to the Criteria's systems perspective, emphasizing the importance of the whole organization and the interdependence of its parts. Nonprescriptive is reflected by the lack of direction in the Criteria about how an organization should respond to any of the questions. Organizations are encouraged to use whatever approaches to foster continuous improvement and innovation are the best "fit" and most effective in their environment and in line with their culture.

In fact, the most compelling evidence of being nonprescriptive is that the Criteria are composed of only questions. There are no declarative statements in the Process and Results items. So, although the Criteria represent a standard against which excellence can be assessed, they are very different from the kind of standards against which organizations are audited or surveyed. Dr. Katherine Gottlieb, CEO of Southcentral Foundation (a Baldrige Award health care recipient in 2011), says, "What I like about Baldrige is that it doesn't tell us what to do. It challenges us to give our own answers."

Another difference is the foundation of the Core Values and Concepts. These were added in 1993. The Criteria are based on "these beliefs and behaviors (that) are embedded in high-performing organizations. They are the foundation for integrating key performance and operational requirements within a results-oriented framework that create a bias for action, feedback, and ongoing success."[6]

For the business, government, and nonprofit Criteria, the Core Values and Concepts are:

- Systems perspective
- Visionary leadership
- Customer-focused excellence
- Valuing people
- Organizational learning and agility
- Focus on success
- Managing for innovation
- Management by fact
- Societal responsibility
- Ethics and transparency
- Delivering value and results

There are some slight variations for the education and health care versions of the Criteria. For example, in health care, customer-focused excellence is replaced with patient-focused excellence. In education, this core value is stated as student-centered excellence.

We frequently show the Core Values and Concepts (Figure 1.2) to executives and ask, "Wouldn't you like to have your organization described in these terms?" The answer is always a resounding, "Yes." Only then do we reveal the source of these powerful phrases.

FIGURE 1.2 Role of Core Values

The Baldrige Criteria build on
core values and concepts ········

which are embedded in
systematic processes...
(Criteria categories 1–6)

yielding
performance results.
(Criteria category 7)

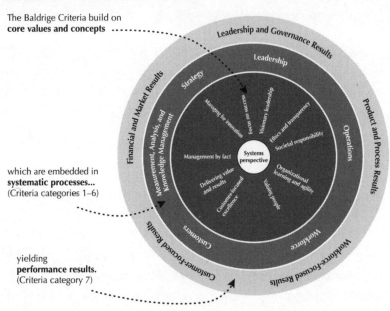

From Baldrige Performance Excellence Program. 2015. *2015–2016 Baldrige Excellence Framework: A Systems Approach to
Improving Your Organization's Performance.* Gaithersburg, MD: U.S. Department of Commerce,
National Institute of Standards and Technology. http://www.nist.gov/baldrige.

An Introduction to Baldrige—Checklist

1. Several leaders cited the advantages they found in using
   the Baldrige Excellence Framework. These included better
   alignment, more consistency, and the value in identifying
   strategic challenges and advantages. How would your organization benefit from these?
2. What new or emerging concepts do think should be added
   to the Criteria?
3. Do the core values of the Baldrige Criteria appeal to you?
   Which ones and why?

Why Employee
Engagement Matters

- What is employee engagement?
- What is the impact of an engaged workforce?
- What are the costs of a disengaged workforce?
- Why don't more senior leaders work harder to engage their employees?

If you enter "employee engagement" as a search in Google, in 0.36 second, you'll get about 7,440,000 results. There seems to be some interest in this topic! Use the same phrase to search for books on the subject, and you'll find there are more than 8,000 titles listed. What makes this book different from those? We decided to look at organizations that have been recognized for excellent performance across multiple dimensions as well as world-class processes to see how employee engagement played a role in achieving these results. These organizations are the recipients of the Malcolm Baldrige National Quality Award or the recipients of programs that are based on the same criteria. What should also be noted is that these organizations represent every sector—manufacturing, service, health care, education, small business, government, and nonprofit—ranging from very large organizations with more than 10,000 employees to those with less than 40. Some of the organizations have a workforce that is represented by one or more bargaining units; others do not. Some are publicly traded, while others are privately held. In short, the common denominator in the organizations we studied is their use of the Baldrige framework as the way they operate.

What Is Employee Engagement?

In our search to better understand what drives engagement, we soon discovered that there are nearly as many opinions about the definition of the term as there are hits in the Google search. Because of the organizations we chose to explore, we opted to use the Baldrige Criteria definition for workforce engagement, "The extent of workforce members' emotional and intellectual commitment to accomplishing your organization's work, mission, and vision. Organizations with high levels of workforce engagement are often . . . environments in which people are motivated to do their utmost for their customers' benefit and the organization's success."[1] Each of the senior leaders we interviewed emphasized the criticality of an engaged workforce to achieving their organization's success. However, the ways that they promoted engagement were often different depending on the challenges faced in their competitive environment and the prevailing culture they encountered if they joined an organization (rather than founding it, as some of the senior leaders we interviewed did).

What Is the Impact of an Engaged Workforce?

A recent report conducted by Harvard Business Review Analytic Services surveying 550 executives found that 71 percent of respondents ranked employee engagement as very important to achieving overall organizational success. However, only 24 percent of the respondents said that employees in their organizations are highly engaged.[2]

Gallup's *State of the Global Workplace* report found that only 30 percent of the employees in the United States are engaged. "Engaged workers stand apart from their non-engaged and actively disengaged counterparts because of the discretionary effort they consistently bring to their roles. These employees willingly go the extra mile, work with passion, and feel a profound connection to their company. They are the people who will drive innovation and move your business forward."[3]

Gallup regularly completes meta-analysis research (a statistical technique that pools multiple studies) on its Q^{12} employee engagement measurement tool. It conducted its eighth meta-analysis in 2012 with data from 263 research studies across 192 organizations in 49 industries and 34 countries. This study included nearly 1.4 million employees. As previous studies had shown, this latest study again confirmed the "well-established connection between employee engagement and key performance outcomes:

- Customer ratings
- Profitability
- Productivity
- Turnover (for both high-turnover and low-turnover types of organizations)
- Safety incidents
- Theft of company materials (shrinkage)
- Absenteeism
- Patient safety incidents
- Quality (defects)"[4]

Kevin Kruse, *New York Times* bestselling author and *Forbes* columnist, cites some impressive statistics. "According to Towers Perrin research, companies with engaged workers have 6% higher net profit margins, and according to Kenexa research, engaged companies have five times higher shareholder returns over five years." The Boston Consulting Group analyzed what it called "People companies"—those that had appeared on *Fortune's* 100 Best Companies to Work For list in at least 3 of the past 10 years—and found these companies outperformed the S&P 500 in 8 of the past 10 years, with an 88 percent higher shareholder return.[5]

Later in the book, we'll present similarly compelling evidence of the link between employee engagement and impressive performance in customer loyalty, profitability, and marketplace success in the organizations profiled.

What Are the Costs of a Disengaged Workforce?

Everyone focuses on the costs of employee turnover, and yes, those are pretty high. Estimates for recruiting, interviewing, hiring, and training coupled with reduced productivity and lost opportunity costs to replace an employee can be staggering.

"For entry-level employees, it costs between 30–50 percent of their annual salary to replace them. For mid-level employees, it costs upward of 150 percent of their annual salary to replace them. For high-level or highly specialized employees, you're looking at 400 percent of their annual salary."[6]

A recent article in *Harvard Business Review* cited these statistics gleaned from other studies. "Disengaged workers had 37% higher absenteeism, 49% more accidents, and 60% more errors and defects. In organizations with low employee engagement scores, they experienced 18% lower productivity, 16% lower profitability, 37% lower job growth, and 65% lower share price over time."[7]

These are huge sums of money that directly affect the bottom line of an organization. However, we suggest that there may be a less obvious but no less significant impact to the bottom line with disengaged employees who *stay* with an organization. And these less visible costs grow exponentially. Disengaged employees aren't going to go the extra mile to satisfy a customer. They aren't going to protect the organization's resources as if they were their own. They aren't going to look for ways to add value. They aren't going to encourage each other to levels of higher productivity. They aren't going to innovate. These types of employees are described below as "captives."

PwC Advisory published its *2015 Employee Engagement Landmark Study: Championing Greatness or Capturing Mediocrity* partly in response to the finding from PwC's 18th Annual Global CEO Survey. "CEOs see more opportunities and growth for their business today than three years ago. While many CEOs are confident about their business direction, most (73%) remain concerned about the availability of key skills to help fuel and sustain this growth."[8] In that same study, they characterize employees into four types of engagement:

- **Champions** are energized and motivated to perform for their company and demonstrate a high desire to remain at the company. They have a strong identification with the organization's objectives and a strong sense of loyalty. They also work collaboratively and help to motivate fellow employees.
- **Tenants** are energized and motivated but less committed to staying than Champions. Some of this may stem from where they are in their career or a desire for next steps not likely available within their current organization.
- **Disconnected** employees aren't motivated to contribute, and they also are not committed to staying with the organization. Unless key roles and top talent

are among the disconnected, it may be enough to help them find their next opportunity—*outside* your organization.

- **Captives** have low levels of engagement but plan to stay with the organization. "These individuals often create the biggest risk within organizations because they're not planning to go anywhere, but they aren't necessarily driven to make a real contribution. This creates a drag on the company's ability to produce and perform."[9]

Why Don't More Senior Leaders Work Harder to Engage Their Employees?

We wonder about that, too. The evidence that employee engagement leads to superior outcomes for an organization isn't in dispute. However, we believe that the personal ambition and egos of many senior leaders are the primary reasons that prevent them from focusing on achieving real employee engagement. In *The Leadership Challenge*, James Kouzes and Barry Posner state, "In many all-too-subtle ways, it's easy to be seduced by power and importance. It's possible for any leader to get infected with the disease of arrogance and pride, becoming bloated with an exaggerated sense of self and pursuing one's own ends."[10]

In his bestselling book, *Good to Great*, Jim Collins offers that "Level 5 leaders embody a paradoxical mix of personal humility and professional will. They are ambitious, to be sure, but ambitious first and foremost for the company, not themselves."[11]

It's probably no coincidence how many of the senior leaders of Baldrige Award recipients we interviewed for this book referred to *Good to Great*, and they certainly displayed this exceptional blend of determination with humbleness. They are quick to give credit to their team of other senior leaders and to their workforce for all that their organizations have accomplished.

At one of his conferences, Michael Hammer said, "The soft stuff is the hard stuff." Quint Studer, founder of the Studer Group (a Baldrige Award recipient in 2010), echoed that sentiment in one of his blog posts, "As we've worked with hundreds of organizations over the year, it has not been unusual to hear senior leaders characterize the ability to maximize employee engagement and patient perception of care (satisfaction) as a 'soft skill.' We've also found that most of the time these comments came from leaders of organizations that are not achieving the results in the people areas they would like to achieve." He went on to explain, "The words we use matter because they determine our actions. Only when an organization's leaders understand that what they call soft skills are actually hard skills will they approach them with the needed focus. And only then will they get the results it takes to thrive in today's challenging environment."[12]

It takes a self-confident leader to admit that she or he doesn't have all the answers. It takes an assured leader to surround himself or herself with people who are smarter and more accomplished. It also takes a leader with the maturity to understand that good ideas can come from anywhere and anyone in the organization. And it takes a really savvy leader to "view employee engagement with the same significance as profitability, customer loyalty and other key business performance measures."[13]

In the coming chapters, we'll let some self-confident leaders share the various ways they promote employee engagement and how that has enabled them and their organizations to succeed. The vision of Malcolm Baldrige in championing the development of a standard of excellence to guide leaders of American organizations has paid enormous dividends for them and for the country.

Why Employee Engagement Matters—Checklist

1. How engaged are your employees? How do you know?
2. How does your workforce engagement compare with the average for your industry? For your competitors?
3. How does your turnover compare with the average for your industry? With the top quartile? How does your turnover compare with that of your competitors?
4. How difficult is it to find qualified candidates for job openings in your organization?
5. What are your biggest challenges to engaging your employees?

Organizational Culture and How It Impacts Employee Engagement

- The importance of vision
- Senior leaders' role with respect to vision
- The link between vision and strategy in engaging employees
- The link between vision and values, recruiting and hiring, and retention
- How the Baldrige framework reinforces the vision

Although the quote "Culture eats strategy for breakfast" has frequently been attributed to Peter Drucker, that fact hasn't been substantiated. However, given Drucker's body of work, it certainly seems like something he might have said. The quote underscores the importance of culture to any organization, regardless of how simple or sophisticated its strategy might be. What we have come to believe through our work on this book is that an organization's culture is the engine that drives the strategy. A high-powered engine can drive strategy aggressively. A weak engine underperforms in any competition.

Every organization has a culture. The question for leaders is, are you intentionally creating and reinforcing that culture with your words and personal actions, or is the culture of your organization merely the by-product of neglect and tolerance for what has taken place over the years? Every leader we interviewed for this book talked about the culture of his or her organization, although we never asked a question specifically about culture. They talked about how their culture related to the organization's vision and mission, how it was shaped by the values, and how it led to engaged and empowered employees.

The Importance of Vision

"Vision is the bigger picture that motivates employees because they understand how their individual efforts contribute to the overall dream," explain Kevin and Jackie Freiberg in *Nuts! Southwest Airlines' Crazy Recipe for Business and Personal Success*.[1] When leaders spend time developing, communicating, and reinforcing a compelling vision statement, the results can be amazing. A clear vision statement is the foundation for employee empowerment and engagement if every individual can determine whether his or her actions are in alignment with the vision for the organization.

What we find in most of the Baldrige Award recipients is a palpable culture that begins with their vision statement (although some organizations refer to it as their mission). It is an intentional versus accidental culture. The senior leaders know exactly the organizational attributes they want their cultures to reflect. Author Jim Collins described it as a "'SMAC' recipe—specific, methodical, and consistent, just like the Baldrige process."[2]

We talked with Dr. Harry Hertz, Director Emeritus of the Baldrige Performance Excellence Program, about this "palpable" culture because we've heard him use that phrase many times. When we asked him to describe the specific characteristics of this type of culture, he laughed and said, "I wish I knew so that we could spray the mist in the air of other organizations. You see it with the smiles on people's faces. The way they walk around the facility—even their gait is different. You see it in the way they interact with you—a visitor—and with each other. There's a celebratory nature where people aren't afraid to tackle problems together. There's a family sort of environment, even with the bigger companies you walk into like the Ritz-Carlton (a two-time Baldrige Award recipient in 1992 and 1999). Maybe it's a culture that's epitomized by understanding and living the organization's core values. Values empower the employees and contribute to that palpable culture."

SSM Health Care, the first health care recipient of the Baldrige Award (2002), spent nearly two years in developing its mission that would ultimately unite all of the system's hospitals and other health care facilities. The senior leaders engaged the workforce at all levels and all areas through multiple focus groups to mine what made SSM Health Care unique. Their simple but memorable mission is, "Through our exceptional health care services, we reveal the healing presence of God."[3] Sister Mary Jean Ryan, FSM, former president and CEO, says, "Best of all, we've figured out how to translate our mission imperative—that is, 'exceptional health care services'—into specific and measurable goals."

Tommy Gonzalez, former city manager for the City of Irving (a Baldrige Award recipient in government in 2012), described responding to feedback he received from employee engagement surveys: "There was a lot going on, but people felt lost. We created a Playbook. These are our 'plays.' These are the Vision, Mission, and Values. Here is our Strategic

Plan. Here are the KPIs [key performance indicators] tied to the plan. Our employees don't just memorize the vision, they understand it. They know they're a part of its success, and they know how that success is measured."

The City of Irving's vision statement is "The City of Irving will be the model for safe and beautiful neighborhoods, a vibrant economy, and exceptional recreational, cultural, and educational opportunities." The power of this vision statement in engaging the workforce was demonstrated during the organization's Baldrige site visit. When one of the examiners asked a city worker who was out picking up trash what he was doing, he proudly announced that he was helping to create a safe and beautiful neighborhood.

At K&N Management (a Baldrige Award small business recipient in 2010), the vision statement, "To Become World Famous By Delighting One Guest at a Time," is supported with a mission that speaks to every employee: "To Guarantee Every Guest is Delighted Because of Me." You might expect such lofty words from the Ritz-Carlton, but would you expect them from an organization of fast-casual restaurants with walk-up counter service and a limited menu? However, all employees at K&N Management, regardless of their position, can describe how they *personally* delight each guest in fulfillment of that vision.

Dr. Katherine Gottlieb, CEO of Southcentral Foundation (SCF) (a Baldrige Award health care recipient in 2011), said, "Baldrige came in and asked the question, 'How does every employee know they are achieving the vision?' We said, 'That's a really good question,' and we didn't have a good answer at first." By the time SCF received its site visit in 2011, every staff member—from receptionists, to health care providers, to maintenance workers—could share how the work he or she does personally contributes to achieving the vision and mission of the organization.

At MidwayUSA (Baldrige Award small business recipient in 2009 and 2015), the vision statement is, "To be the best-run, most respected business in America, for the benefit of our Customers." This bold statement is made by a small family-owned catalog and Internet retailer based in Columbia, Missouri. On a recent trip there to tour the operations and meet with senior leaders and employees, every person we spoke with articulated what the vision meant to her or him and how it impacted their daily actions. Matt Fleming, the president of MidwayUSA, says, "If you have the right vision and the right people, you're practically guaranteed to get the right things done."

On the same tour, Larry Potterfield, founder and CEO of MidwayUSA, proudly introduced us to the organization's latest approach to reinforce its values. We watched groups of employees etching the values in numerous places on sidewalks across the campus and at the entrance of each of the four buildings (Figure 3.1). This innovative approach ensures that every employee, customer, or visitor who walks around MidwayUSA is reminded of the organization's "Concrete Values" (Figure 3.2).

Jayne Pope, CEO, Hill Country Memorial (HCM) (2014 Baldrige Award recipient in health care), describes how the Baldrige journey challenged her organization to rethink its vision. "Before we engaged with the Baldrige Criteria, we thought we wanted to be the best community hospital anywhere. And then we started using the Baldrige Criteria, and we started to dream bigger. We thought about being the best hospital in the nation." The organization also took an intentional approach to defining its values.

Alysha Metzger, director of human resources, described how the organization put together a 31-person team that included multiple levels of leaders, team members, physicians, and community members to identify HCM's values—others

FIGURE 3.1 MidwayUSA's Employees Etching the Values

first, compassion, innovation, accountability, and steward-
ship. Then the team took the values, still in draft form, on
a "listening tour" to every department and every shift, as
well as to community members. They also defined the min-
imum expected behaviors for each value for which every
staff member and vendor would be held accountable. Physicians on the team defined these for themselves and their
peers.[4]

Senior Leaders' Role with Respect to Vision

In *The Leadership Challenge*, James Kouzes and Barry Posner
state, "Leaders help people see that what they are doing is bigger than they are and bigger, even, than the business. Their
work can be something noble. When people go to bed at night,
they can sleep a little easier knowing that others are able
to live a better life because of what they did that day."[5] The

FIGURE 3.2   MidwayUSA's "Concrete Values"

senior leaders interviewed for this book certainly understood this principle and demonstrated it.

Paul Worstell, retired CEO of PRO-TEC Coating Company (a Baldrige Award small business recipient in 2007), says, "We need to tie everything we do to the Mission, Vision, and Values [MVV] and to our strategies." When he communicated his intent to start the company on a Baldrige journey, he told his senior leadership team, "This change is going to be uncomfortable for a while, but it's essential we do this. We need to create a line of sight to the MVV when we communicate with the rest of the organization."

When asked what he did that he would replicate if he were to lead another Baldrige journey, Paul stated, "Emphasizing the importance of the Mission, Vision, and Values." Reflecting the permanence of MidwayUSA's "Concrete Values," Paul took a similar approach. "Immediately paint the MVV on the walls, in conference rooms, in hallways, and in work stations. By painting them, you're declaring that these are permanent— not something we can hang up and take down." They used these to create a line of sight between the frontline associates and the higher purpose "to where a mechanic isn't think- ing, 'I just turn bolts.' He's thinking, 'I'm manufacturing the best steel in America—saving energy and saving lives'" (see Appendix A for a link to a video about the PRO-TEC Coating Company culture).

Dale Crownover, CEO of Texas Nameplate Company, Inc. (a Baldrige Award small business recipient in 1998 and 2004), talked about how the Baldrige approach is so much more than your products. "It's that plus everything else. It's the big pic- ture—learning, systems, and processes. What Baldrige will do for the workforce is to excite them to see the big picture— they're not just making nameplates."

Because the senior leaders at AtlantiCare (a Baldrige Award recipient in health care in 2009) originally planned to use the Baldrige framework as a leadership tool, they had not given the workforce much information about it. David Tilton, CEO, shared that after their first site visit, "Our staff came to us and said, 'We want to understand what this is about. We want to participate, and we think we could add value.'"

AtlantiCare developed an explicit approach to connect every employee with the "big dots" of the organization, the 5Bs (Best People and Workplace, Best Customer Service, Best Quality, Best Growth, and Best Financial Performance). These are cascaded down through the organization using a strategy map that "connects the dots" of the 5Bs to every employee through individual performance excellence commitments. The organization has continued to use this approach since receiving the Baldrige Award in 2009. David shared that he had recently given a performance update to the board. "We hit our stretch goals for three of the Bs and achieved the target for the remaining two Bs. In our recent employee engagement survey, it's been our third straight time to be in the top decile, and this year we're in the top 5 percent of our peer group. If I had to attribute our success to one thing, it's an engaged workforce. They can run through walls!"

The Link Between Vision and Strategy in Engaging Employees

"Alignment between the vision and the strategy is so important," says Tommy Gonzalez, former city manager of the City of Irving (a Baldrige Award government recipient in 2012). "Most organizations don't really understand that 'alignment' word. That was why our Playbook was so important. It got all of our senior leaders and managers on the same page, understanding how everybody was contributing to the overall goals of the organization."

In his book *Customer Culture: How FedEx and Other Great Companies Put the Customer First Every Day*, former senior vice president at FedEx (a Baldrige Award service recipient in 1990) Michael Basch says, "You'd be surprised. Empowered people with a clear purpose and direction will always go further to serve their customers and make you a profit than you could ever ask them or tell them to."[6]

Jayne Pope, CEO of Hill Country Memorial (a Baldrige Award health care recipient in 2014), says, "How do you manage to make the complex, simple? We pride ourselves on that. Our strategy map is posted on the walls of our hospital and on our website [Figure 3.3]. Every team member can tell you how they fit into that."

The senior leaders at Charleston Area Medical Center (CAMC) (a 2015 Baldrige Award recipient) talk about an

FIGURE 3.3   Hill Country Memorial's 2015–2017 Strategy Map

VISION: Empower others. Create healthy.   MISSION: Remarkable always.

FOCUS	ALWAYS GOALS	OBJECTIVES	BALANCED SCORECARD				
			INITIATIVES	MEASURE OF SUCCESS	2015 GOAL	2017 GOAL	LEAD
FINANCE + GROWTH	Embrace and drive remarkable patient value and increase profitability	F1 Strengthen Financial Independence	Achieve Strong Income Statement, Balance Sheet, and Cash Flow	Financial Flexibility Index	Achieve 89th %ile	Achieve 90th %ile	Mark Jones
				Productivity—Action OI	Achieve 50th %ile	Achieve 45th %ile	Mike Reno
		F2 Maximize Key Business Opportunities	Expand our Health Care Boundaries	Market Share			Mark Jones
				Revenue Growth			Debbye Dooley Steve Pfeiffer / Debbye Dooley Emily Padula
SERVICE	Deliver a remarkable experience to exceed expectations	S1 Achieve Engagement Through Relationships	Benchmark and Implement World-Class Service	Patient Satisfaction	Achieve 96th %ile on all benchmarked surveys	Maintain 97th %ile on all bench marked surveys	Maureen Polvika
				Patient Experience (CAHPS)	HCAHPS – Achieve 96th %ile on all categories	HCAHPS – Achieve 97th %ile on all categories	Maureen Polvika
					HHCAHPS – Achieve 92nd %ile on all categories	HHCAHPS – Achieve 95th %ile on all categories	Emily Padula
QUALITY	Redefine health care for increased patient value	Q1 Provide Remarkable Health Care	Eliminate Preventable Harm	Risk Adjusted Mortality Rate	Achieve 90th %ile	Achieve >90th %ile	Jim Partin
			Identify, Evaluate, and Implement Best Practices	Risk Adjusted Complication Rate	Achieve 90th %ile	Achieve >90th %ile	Jim Partin
				Value Based Purchasing Score	Achieve a 5% improvement over baseline in VBP score	Achieve a 5% improvement over baseline in VBP score	Emily Padula
		Q2 Improve Community Health	Partner to Address Community Needs	Community Health Action Plan	75% of 2013-2015 Community Health Action Plan	25% of 2016-2019 Community Health Action Plan Goals Achieved	Emily Padula
PEOPLE	Be a team of champions	P1 Develop a High Performance Team	Recruit, Retain, and Promote Champions	Workforce Turnover (TO)	Achieve 90th%ile Employee VTO	Achieve >90th %ile Employee VTO	Jayne Pope
					Improve Volunteer VTO by 5% over 2014	Improve Volunteer VTO by 10% over 2014	Mike Reno
				Workforce Engagement	Achieve 92nd %ile on Employee willingness to recommend	Achieve 95th %ile on Employee willingness to recommend	Jayne Pope
					Achieve 90th %ile on Physician willingness to recommend	Achieve >90th %ile on Physician willingness to recommend	Jim Partin

INNOVATION   SERVICE EXCELLENCE   OPERATIONAL EXCELLENCE

KEY WORK SYSTEM REQUIREMENTS

HCM | HILL COUNTRY MEMORIAL

C

34

important element in their journey to performance excellence: their goal cascade process that links every employee with the strategic objectives of the organization. Like Atlanti-Care, CAMC takes its strategic plan to identify the "Big Dots" that are cascaded down through the organization and ultimately result in goals on each employee's performance plan.

The Link Between Vision, Recruiting and Hiring, and Retention

At K&N Management, the recruiting process prominently features the mission of the organization. It's front and center on the online application website. Applicants are assessed for alignment with the organization's core values—Excellence | Quality | Integrity | Relationships—during the interview process. Every new team member goes through a one-day Foundations course taught at the corporate office where the vision, mission, and core values as well as standards and expectations are communicated. The culture is reinforced daily through frontline communication, coaching, and performance feedback.

Allyson Young, HR and brand director at K&N Management, has said, "We can't achieve our mission or vision without the best people. If you don't spend the resources to select, train, engage, and retain the best people, you or your managers will spend the majority of their time and energy dealing with workforce issues. We strive to treat our workforce as our internal customers, build relationships, and create an experience for them that will leave them delighted."[7] In other words, they apply the same principle of their mission to external and internal customers.

Stan Frink, VP of human resources at MidwayUSA, says, "Our interview process is aligned with the culture and the values. We're not as interested in the technical skills as the applicant's alignment with the values. And if you don't buy into Baldrige, you won't fit in here." Matt Fleming, President of MidwayUSA, is even more emphatic. "Don't misunderstand the amount of energy you waste if you don't hire the right people." To ensure that every candidate for salaried positions is right for the MidwayUSA culture, the final interview is conducted by two members of the career development team, which is composed of senior leaders. Matt also describes the culture to the candidates this way: "If you hate change, you're going to hate it here. We're all about change and continuous improvement."

In a meeting with some relatively new employees at MidwayUSA, we asked how they described their orientation and the culture. "It's not a destination, but a journey. Baldrige is the way we eat, drink, sleep, and run the business." Another added, "But after orientation, the senior leaders don't talk about Baldrige, per se. You just see it by the way we operate."

Gerry Agnes, CEO of Elevations Credit Union (a Baldrige Award nonprofit recipient in 2014), says that being on the Baldrige journey has created a great employee value proposition, which is "Elevations is the best place you've ever worked!" "We've even shared our state and Baldrige applications with potential job applicants. It's a great recruiting tool." Jay Campion, COO at Elevations Credit Union, shared at the 2015 Quest for Excellence® conference that 25 percent of employees' performance evaluations is based on their adherence to the organization's core values, which further reinforces alignment.

Multiple senior leaders described the importance of their personal participation in new employee orientation where new workforce members are introduced to the organization's mission, vision, and values. Scott McIntyre, managing partner, PricewaterhouseCoopers Public Sector Practice (a Baldrige Award service recipient in 2014), says about his role in teaching a portion of their new employee orientation, "It's easy to talk about what you will do or won't do because of our values. When an issue presents itself, that's when you can show the organization why you're not deviating from your vision and values. I give very specific examples where short-term opportunities have been forgone to stick to our values." Larry Potterfield and Matt Fleming of MidwayUSA and most of the other leaders we interviewed also personally speak at every new employee orientation about the vision, mission, and values.

How the Baldrige Framework Reinforces the Vision

The Baldrige Criteria reinforce the importance of vision by asking for the mission, vision, and values as part of the Organizational Profile, which establishes the context for examiners as they begin to review an application. Then the Criteria ask how the senior leaders have set the vision and values, how they deploy them throughout their leadership system to the workforce, key suppliers and partners, key customers, and other stakeholders. One powerful question is, "How do senior leaders' *personal* actions reflect a commitment to those values?"[8]

Under Leadership and Governance Results, the Criteria ask about the results for key measures or indicators "of senior leaders' communication and engagement with the workforce and customers to deploy" the vision and values.

Dr. Joe Alexander, former dean of the Kenneth W. Monfort College of Business (a Baldrige Award education recipient in 2004), described the college's first feedback report from the Baldrige-based state program and first site visit. "It was something like this, 'Great Mission, Vision, and Values and good results. You just don't know what happens in the black box in between them.'" The power of that feedback led Joe and his senior leaders to identify the processes that delivered the results in support of the vision. He went on to explain, "Baldrige forced us to formalize the processes. In between the first and second year of submitting our applications, we understood what we did or did not do. And where there were gaps, we developed the processes to close them. Even after earning the award, for the next two years (I was at the school), we kept getting better."

Organizational Culture and How It Impacts Employee Engagement—Checklist

1. How would you characterize the culture of your organization? Is that the culture you want to have? If not, what do you need to do to start changing it?
2. How do you communicate your organization's vision and values to help your workforce feel that they are serving a "noble purpose"?
3. What are the actions that you and your senior leaders take that demonstrate your personal commitment to your organization's values?
4. How do you connect every employee's work with the highest-level objectives of the organization?
5. How can you use your organization's values and culture to make better hiring decisions?
6. What is your personal role in new employee orientation?

Drivers of Employee Engagement

- How high-performing organizations determine employee engagement
- The importance of trust in senior leaders to employee engagement
- How senior leaders use employee engagement surveys to foster employee engagement

In doing research for this book, we reviewed more than a dozen large studies regarding employee engagement. In these, we found respondents categorized by country, by industry, by gender, by generation, and by other interesting segments. However, even selecting one of these groups for comparison, we found no generally accepted drivers of employee engagement. That might have been troubling, but one factor did surface in the majority of the reports we reviewed—confidence in senior leadership. Factors contributing to high ratings for confidence in senior leadership were their perceived trustworthiness, their ability to effectively communicate the vision of the organization in ways that allowed the employees to see how they contribute, and their demonstration of sincere interest in the well-being of employees. In fact, in one study, the leadership driver is by far the strongest, having nearly one-third more impact on employee engagement than the next three strongest drivers.[1]

Because of their importance to employee engagement, this book has focused exclusively on the actions senior leaders of Baldrige Award recipients and recipients of Baldrige-based awards took to promote a culture of high performance. However, these approaches should be useful for leaders throughout an organization—regardless of title—to bring an entire organization along the journey to performance excellence. John Kotter offers a simple military analogy: "A peacetime army can usually survive with good administration and management up and down the hierarchy, coupled with good leadership at the very top. A wartime army, however, needs competent leadership at all levels. No one yet has figured out how to manage people effectively into battle; they must be led."[2]

How High-Performing Organizations Determine Employee Engagement

As with other key processes, senior leaders of Baldrige Award recipient organizations assess employee engagement systematically. All leaders interviewed for this book stated that they had for years conducted annual or biennial employee satisfaction and engagement surveys. Some augment that information with intermittent "pulse" surveys of a random sample of employees. We found this practice even more compelling when we read that companies that survey employees on a regular basis (at least every other year) report about 50 percent of their employees falling into the Champion category (Chapter 2) versus only 29 percent among those who don't regularly survey their employees or survey them at all.[3]

In addition to formal surveys, smart leaders also use informal ways to assess workforce engagement. They observe attendance at voluntary meetings and events. They look for employee participation in offering suggestions or making recommendations for how to improve the way work is done. They look for collaboration among work groups. And they monitor other leading indicators of engagement such as attendance, safety, and grievances. In short, they don't wait for a year or two to transpire to get a sense of how engaged their employees are, so they can take corrective action if needed.

As many senior leaders reminded us when we asked about their use of surveys, it isn't sufficient to simply ask the questions. Leaders need to analyze the data from the surveys, share the results with the workforce, and solicit their input for identifying and prioritizing what to address.

The Importance of Trust in Senior Leaders to Employee Engagement

The trustworthiness of senior leaders is assessed on multiple levels. On a personal level, these include leaders being ethical and behaving in accordance with an organization's stated values. Another is the credibility, consistency, and openness of senior leaders' communication. Employees want to know that what they are told is the truth and that they are not kept in the dark about issues affecting the organization, the industry, and their own future. Another level of trust stems from the belief that senior leaders genuinely care about their employees as individuals, not just the labor costs required to provide a product or render a service.

In a 2014 survey conducted by Tolero Solutions, 45 percent of employees cited their lack of trust in leadership— executives and managers—as having the biggest negative impact on their performance at work.[4] A lack of trust in leaders results in many things that cause overall organizational performance to decline. If employees don't believe that senior leaders tell them the truth about what is happening in the organization, a lot of time is spent speculating and trying to protect their self-interests rather than those of the organization. Neither of these is productive. In addition, if the workforce doesn't trust that senior leaders genuinely care about them as individuals, they will not offer information and ideas that could benefit the organization. Stephen M. R. Covey puts it this way, "When trust is low, in a company or in a relationship, it places a hidden 'tax' on every transaction: every communication, every interaction, every strategy, every decision is taxed, bringing speed down and sending costs up. My experience is that significant distrust doubles the cost of doing business and triples the time it takes to get things done."[5]

Some of the ways that the senior leaders featured in this book build trust with their employees are discussed in Chapter 5, "Using Data to Drive Engagement"; Chapter 7, "Maintaining Momentum When Facing a Downturn"; and Chapter 11, "Confronting a Culture of Entitlement."

How Senior Leaders Use Employee Engagement Surveys to Foster Employee Engagement

Dr. Rulon Stacey, former CEO of Poudre Valley Health System (a 2008 Baldrige Award recipient), shared some of his experience regarding the importance of assessing employee engagement and acting on the feedback. "When I joined Poudre Valley, a group of employees met with me about how we [senior leaders] demonstrated we did or did not care about them. They pointed out that we conducted an employee engagement survey every 36 months while we reviewed our financials every 30 days. Their conclusion was that senior leaders were 36 times more concerned about the dollars than we were about our employees."

Rulon went to a previous Baldrige Award recipient, Wainwright Industries, to benchmark its best practices for employee engagement. One key learning was that he needed to get his senior leaders on board with focusing on employee engagement. "You can't engage your employees without the leaders being fully vested in this. I told them, 'Your service to the company is management, and the customers are the employees.'" They began to survey the employees more often until the frequency was twice a year, and the *employees* asked them to reduce that to annual surveys.

The process that followed the survey was that anyone who supervised anyone had to review the feedback from his or her group, have a face-to-face meeting with the employees of the group, and say, "I've read the feedback, and this is where I think I can do better. What do you think?" Then the agreed-upon action plan would be posted for everyone to see. Even Rulon followed the same process and posted his action plan. He gave an example of feedback he received: "Rulon has a tendency when he's out talking to people to make decisions without involving us. We think that undermines our roles. Before he commits the organization, he needs to come back to the senior leaders for us to discuss it." Rulon acknowledged that they were right and included changing his behavior in his action plan.

Another lesson the senior leaders of Poudre Valley Health System learned came from attending a Studer Group meeting where data were shared showing that the greatest source of employee dissatisfaction came from not having adequate access to the supervisor. The research also showed that the optimum span of control was about 15 subordinates. In calculating what it would take to achieve that span of control, Rulon went to the board and got its approval to hire 60 additional managers. He was able to gain the board's approval for such a large investment through the research data and the

costs the organization was incurring from the high turnover resulting from employee dissatisfaction. He estimates
that turnover for one nurse cost the organization some-
where between $200,000 and $300,000. There was also the
acknowledgment that longer-tenured nurses provided better
care. With the addition of the 60 new managers, turnover
went down. Rulon said, "We simultaneously drove costs down
and quality up. Reducing turnover accomplishes both of these
important objectives."

Matt Fleming, president of MidwayUSA (a Baldrige Award
recipient in 2009 and 2015), described at a recent Baldrige-
based conference the importance of the top executive owning
the employee engagement survey and the process for analyzing and addressing the feedback. In July 2011, the company
wasn't achieving the levels of employee satisfaction and
engagement it wanted. He asked the senior leaders to write
down their responses as to the causes. The answers were all
over the map and were not fact-based. He felt that a big part
of the problem was that the senior leaders had delegated the
employee engagement survey and response to the feedback to
the human resources department.

The company started over, building an anonymous, online
employee engagement survey instrument from scratch. In it,
the employees are asked to rank order their motivation from
among 14 key requirements of engagement. (These have been
identified over time and are annually reevaluated and revised
as needed.) They may select all, some, or only one of these
requirements. Then, they are asked to assign a percentage to
the key requirements they selected indicating what weight
that particular requirement has on their engagement for a
total of 100 percent. Finally, they use a slider to indicate their
level of satisfaction with each requirement. An open text
field for each selected requirement allows employees to provide individual feedback. The results are tabulated and made

available to the senior leaders within one week of the completion of the survey.

The appropriate survey frequency was determined using feedback from the employees. The company now surveys twice a year, and although the survey is not mandatory, the last survey had a 94 percent response rate. In addition, in a company of about 400 employees, the survey responses included more than 1,600 comments. Matt read every single one of them.

To underscore the importance of leadership in owning the employee engagement process, Matt personally moderates every focus group of employees. He conducts eight (one for each work group) with a random selection of nine employees from that work group. He shared, "You have to create a safe environment where people can tell the president of the company exactly what they think. You have to prove that you are there to listen, learn, and improve. And if you're really listening, they shouldn't have to tell you the same thing multiple times in the survey or in the focus groups. What we have also learned is that you have to keep improving to even maintain a score because the expectations rise."

David Ramsey, CEO of Charleston Area Medical Center (a 2015 Baldrige Award recipient), talked about how the organization's employee survey process has improved during its journey. "We have more participation. The process is more rigorous with departments and department managers being expected to discuss the feedback with their groups and act on it. As a result of that expectation, some managers no longer work here. And that's been a positive thing." Such action certainly demonstrated the top executive's ownership of the process and commitment to employee engagement!

Drivers of Employee Engagement—Checklist

1. Do your employees trust you and your senior leaders? How do you know?
2. How do you and your senior leaders demonstrate that you care about your employees as individuals?
3. Do you conduct employee engagement surveys? If not, why not?
4. Who owns the employee engagement process?
5. What do you do with employee feedback?

Using Data to Drive Engagement

- Advancing an organization that traditionally has had little data and measures
- The value of comparisons and benchmarks
- Using data to promote healthy competition
- Using data to drive ownership of the organization's performance

The importance of transparency in promoting employee engagement is becoming well documented. Some of this may be due to the changing demographics of the workplace, with millennials entering the workforce in droves. With them come their expectations for what is required to engage them, and transparency is at the top of their list. In 2013, TINYpulse analyzed more than 40,000 anonymous survey responses from over 300 companies around the world. The most surprising result of all was that management transparency is the top factor when it comes to determining employee happiness. And not by just a little. The correlation coefficient between perceived management transparency and employee happiness was a staggering 0.93.[1]

Transparency in leadership includes communicating the why behind what might be an unpopular decision rather than just demanding compliance with it. Transparency is characterized by what the Baldrige Criteria refer to as "frank, two-way communication" between senior leaders and the workforce. And it also includes behaving in consistent, predictable ways.

We can sense the pushback already. Some leaders work in highly competitive environments that make such transparency seem risky. Some may lack sophisticated IT systems that would enable real-time sharing of information. And some just don't think employees need to know everything about the business. Some or all of that may be true, but it doesn't mean that some elements of transparency can't be improved to help employees see how what they do every day matters, how their actions connect to a larger view, and how they contribute to the success of your organization. As TINYpulse founder and CEO, David Niu points out, "Transparency is one of the quickest fixes any leader or manager can make. And it is as free or near-free as you can get."[2]

This also ties to one of the nine critical leadership behaviors that drive employee satisfaction and commitment that we outlined in Chapter 2—trust. It isn't just about being transparent with information; it's also about being credible. When employees "know that they would never be told anything that is not 100 percent accurate and factual, they trust that leader."[3]

As we'll learn from some of the leaders of Baldrige Award recipient organizations, sometimes the earlier lack of transparency in their organizations had been the result of an inadequate data and measurement system. In some cases, the data had been manipulated because of the prevailing punitive environment for not "making the numbers." In other cases, the world was a happier place when the organization didn't have to confront how poor its performance was relative to others. And in still other cases, it might have been uncomfortable for senior leaders to let employees be able to assess the health of the organization for themselves.

Advancing an Organization That Traditionally Has Had Little Data and Measures

You'd think that a financial institution would be rife with data and measurement, right? We certainly believed that until we spoke with Gerry Agnes, CEO of Elevations Credit Union (a Baldrige Award nonprofit recipient in 2014). He describes his surprise when he first joined the organization. "I was shocked at how well the organization had done without a lot of data. We had the financial data, of course, but we didn't have in-process measures, market data, and benchmark data. Developing our data and measurement system along with Business Process Management [BPM] was the biggest contributing factor that changed the culture of the organization." The organization also invested in technology to enable the collection and reporting of more data, including approval by the board of directors to invest $10 million to install a new operating system that went live in 2011.

The organization had not been sufficiently transparent before but, with data, became exceedingly transparent. At first, the data pointed out that the organization was not performing very well in areas that impacted customer satisfaction. "This was uncomfortable for a lot of people, but it enabled us to have difficult conversations when we were having problems serving our credit union members." The senior leaders also had to demonstrate that the data would not be used in a punitive way but as a source of information that would lead to process improvement.

For years, the Credit Union had been measuring employee engagement. One of the questions focused on trust in senior leadership, one of the critical leadership behaviors in driving employee engagement. The results weren't that great. Gerry explained, "If you don't have data, people don't understand why decisions get made. They get attributed to an individual or the result of someone's personality. Data were critical to seeing improvement in employee engagement. If the trust isn't there, the rest of the questions on the employee engagement survey don't matter." At the 2015 Baldrige Quest for Excellence®, he explained further, "To make progress . . . we had to get to the source of truth. My measure of my own success as a leader is, 'Have I created a safe environment for our team to have brutally honest conversations about salient matters that impact our members, employees, and community—that we can handle the truth?'" When an environment like that is created, people have no need to manipulate the data to make the numbers look good.

For the results of creating a culture that used data to drive improvement, see Chapter 12 for Elevations Credit Union's impressive results for employee engagement and credit union member satisfaction.

In *Good to Great*, Jim Collins offers the same observation. The good-to-great leaders created "a culture wherein people had a tremendous opportunity to be heard and, ultimately, for the truth to be heard."[4]

Dr. Bruce Kintz, CEO of Concordia Publishing House (a Baldrige Award nonprofit recipient in 2011), came to the publishing arm of the Lutheran Church—Missouri Synod from a long career with McDonnell Douglas. He was used to having data—and lots of it—at his fingertips. That wasn't the case with his new organization. He determined that the critical measures for his new organization were cost, cycle time, quality, and customer satisfaction. Using a very unsophisticated, low-tech approach, the organization began posting paper copies of these results in plastic holders on a "metric wall" in the executive conference center.

After the implementation of a new ERP (enterprise resource planning) system, Bruce realized that the system could collect and report the data without any manipulation of them, so there could be no "gaming" of the results. Then the system was automated, so there was no human intervention at all. The charts were automatically populated, and automated rules provided red, yellow, and green traffic lights to indicate performance.

Bruce said, "When we started having data at the working level, process ownership went way up. The workforce also owned the data for the processes." People hold themselves accountable to improving their game when they can see the score.

The Value of Comparisons and Benchmarks

If you read a headline on the front page of the sports section in your local newspaper, what would you think if it read, "(Your favorite football team) scored 20 points?" You'd probably be pretty frustrated. Who did the team play, and what did the other team score? In other words, how did your favorite team do against a competitor?

We've heard many senior leaders complain about how difficult it is to get relevant comparative data, and in some cases it is. However, excellent leaders refuse to stop with that excuse. They are relentless in pursuing comparisons and benchmarks because they know that is the only way to truly assess their organizations' performance and relative competitive position.

Sister Mary Jean Ryan, the former CEO of SSM Health Care, the first health care recipient of the Baldrige Award (2002), often describes her biggest "aha" moment in the four years of submitting Baldrige applications as follows: "The examiners acknowledged that our mission statement ('Through our exceptional health care services, we reveal the healing presence of God.') was indeed great—exceptional, even. But they asked us two questions: 'What do you mean by "exceptional"?' And, 'If you want to be exceptional, why are you content to compare yourselves to average?' Those two questions stopped us in our tracks."[5]

The senior leaders then devoted their next cycle of strategic planning to defining "exceptional" and determining how to measure it. The organization went from having best-in-class benchmarks only for operating margins to best-in-class benchmarks for clinical outcomes; patient, employee, and physician satisfaction; and financial performance.

Southcentral Foundation (a Baldrige Award health care recipient in 2011) has found that increasing the use of performance measures, comparisons, and benchmarks has engaged employees to monitor how they and the overall organization are doing against shared goals. When the employees see that a performance gap is emerging in one of the key measures, they are motivated to initiate an improvement effort.

The Studer Group (a Baldrige Award small business recipient in 2010) describes how using the Baldrige Criteria forced it to do better benchmarking on a much deeper level than it had before. Founder and CEO Quint Studer shared, "It also meant that every employee had to become knowledgeable about measurement and benchmarking, and become an expert in process improvement." When the organization began to get its employees involved in measurement and process improvement, "that's what got them excited—when they see that their work is getting better."

Brenda Grant, chief strategy officer of Charleston Area Medical Center (CAMC) (a 2015 Baldrige Award recipient), responded very quickly when we asked what she would do differently if leading another organization on the journey. "I would require people to compare our organization to benchmark results earlier." Dr. Glenn Crotty, COO at CAMC, added, "Over time we matured quite a bit and were able to find multiple data sources for comparisons. It really challenged us when we could see that better performance was possible. We developed processes for setting benchmarks and started displaying our results against the seventieth and ninetieth percentile. It took a while to convince the organization that we needed to display data that way, but ultimately it drove our improvement efforts to achieve great results."

Lockheed Martin Missiles and Fire Control (MFC) (a Baldrige Award recipient in the manufacturing category in 2012) sets very aggressive targets across a wide range of measures. It has also established a culture of never being satisfied with its own performance, and one of the ways it communicates that is by turning the measures on its dashboard red as soon as they have met a target that is considered exceptionally good in the industry. Jim Berry, former president of MFC, said, "Red is good. Our 'reds' are our competitors' greens."

Using Data to Drive Healthy Competition

Some organizations have found ways to leverage the competitive nature in many of us to promote improvement and spark innovation. For example, one of BaldrigeCoach's clients is a large health care system with four hospitals. When system leaders noticed a spike in central line associated blood stream infections (CLABSI), they began posting the number of days on each hospital's units since their last CLABSI occurrence. This was a metric that had real meaning to the workforce trying to deliver the best care. It reminded them to always do the right, evidence-based things to prevent CLABSI. In trying to achieve the best record, the hospitals collaborated while they "competed" to understand the evidence-based practices that had been implemented. In this case, the reward for improved performance was the staff members' pride at providing better care for their patients.

In other cases, the reward can be tangible—a gift card, an article of clothing with the organization's name and logo, or a pizza party. However, we have seen that in many instances, it is the act of the senior leader's personal recognition rather than the size of the award that leads to a more engaged work group.

At K&N Management (a Baldrige Award small business recipient in 2010), leaders found that technology enhanced their use of data and measurement. It allowed them to increase the amount of data collected, increased the segmentation available, and increased the speed at which the data were available. "K&N's management team consists of the two owners, seven senior leaders or directors, and the general managers of *Rudy's* and *Mighty Fine* locations. The group meets each month to monitor key measures." Ken Schiller, co-owner and cofounder of K&N Management, says, "If something is impacting our guests, we pay attention to it."[6]

The use of data increased employee engagement and promoted healthy competition among the stores. There is a monthly performance excellence award given based on performance against 38 different measures tied to key business drivers. Ken says, "We get the behavior that we want through the incentives for the store management team and the employees." Normally, employees receive a 50-percent discount on purchases at the stores. For the store receiving the monthly award, employees eat free all month. Free food, in recognition for performance achievements, can also drive employee engagement!

Using Data to Drive Ownership of the Organization's Performance

At MidwayUSA (a Baldrige Award small business recipient in 2009 and 2015), all employees have access to a wide range of information, including company sales and profits. The engagement this promotes is evident from employee comments we heard, such as: "We measure so many things. It's easy to see the results of our work. It's easy to be engaged when I can see how what I do affects this measure." "Processes for the sake of processes can be boring. Phenomenal results can be exciting!" "People who leave because of all of the measures and documentation, they miss the systematic approach. They go from a proactive culture to a reactive culture where everyone is just flying by the seat of their pants."

How does the company use data to drive accountability along with demonstrating its value of "respect for others"? One of the managers told us, "One of my measures is 'red' right now. I haven't been fired. I haven't been screamed at. We know we have the right people, so we know we have a problem in the system or the process." Once again, when the culture is not punitive, people have no need to manipulate the numbers, and everyone can trust the integrity of the data.

Dr. Rulon Stacey, former CEO of Poudre Valley Health System (now part of University of Colorado Health) (a 2008 Baldrige Award recipient), talked about how transparency was key to accelerating the improvement in the organization. "You've got to get the entire organization committed to and looking at the measures. We began sharing all of our customer satisfaction data, employees' evaluations of their supervisors, our financials. We had transparency across the whole organization." What resulted was employees at all levels, in all departments, taking ownership for the results of the organization.

Ken Schnitzer, chairman of Park Place Dealerships (the parent organization of Park Place Lexus, which won the Baldrige Award in 2005), said that one of things he would do differently in his journey was to share more data—and earlier—with the organization's members (how they refer to their employees). He said, "We're a privately held company. It was against my nature to share a lot of information, particularly financial, with more than a few people. We learned we had to share data with our members to get them involved in making improvements. They also took pride in seeing the impact of what they had accomplished."

We asked how sharing more information had helped the organization maintain its momentum when the economic downturn hit. Ken said, "I wrote a letter to all of the members and told them we had three strengths: good balance sheet, great products, and great people. Then I asked for their help in reducing expenses." The managers met with their work groups and encouraged them to come up with ideas. One idea was replacing the bottled water for customers and members with a water filtering system. That idea alone saved the company hundreds of thousands of dollars and also was an environmentally better solution.

Ken also described a cultural change that occurred during the company's Baldrige journey. "When we recognize we have a problem based on what the data are saying, we don't blame people. We know we have a process breakdown, and we know how to fix that."

Dr. Glenn Crotty (CAMC) talked about how the presentation of data really drove employee ownership for improvement. "We also put our data into a program that presented SPC [statistical process control] charts. That way we could identify when there was special cause variation and address it or when what we were seeing was common cause variation and know when to not tamper with the process."

David Ramsey, CEO at CAMC, describes the organization's process of using data to increase employee engagement. Leaders take their strategic plan to create the "big dots" (the most important strategic objectives) to cascade the goals down to the "Top 5" boards that are posted publicly in every department. Dave said, "We're a pretty transparent organization. You'd be hard-pressed to find employees who don't understand the financials. We're in an environment where many patients don't pay the cost of their care. Our employees understand how they contribute to saving costs and finding more efficient ways to do things." Glenn continued, "The Top 5 boards aren't just boards. They're eight feet by eight feet, and they're displayed where the public can see them, which adds to the transparency. The top five goals for any department are color-coded on every shift, and they're either red or green. Anything that's red requires the department to develop and post an action plan. You'll see the managers and staff huddle in front of the boards. This really engages the staff in improving and addressing the problems."

The more organizations we work with, the more we see the importance of developing metrics that align with the most important objectives of the organization, cascading those throughout the organization, and making progress visible. Not only does sharing data and information with employees demonstrate transparency, which promotes trust in senior leaders, it encourages the workforce to take ownership for impacting the progress toward achieving the most important objectives.

Using Data to Drive Engagement—Checklist

1. How transparent are you and your senior leaders in communicating information to your workforce? What would your employees say?
2. Do you "trust" your employees with data and information that lets them see how the organization is performing?
3. Can your employees quantify the impact of their work—in terms of both financial outcomes and customer satisfaction?
4. How do you display your organization's performance results?
5. How often do your employees spontaneously offer ideas for improving the effectiveness and efficiency of your operations?
6. If you can't share certain information, do you communicate why you can't disclose it at that time?

When You're Already a Pretty Good Organization

- When you think you're already a winner
- When you are a successful organization with no burning platform for change
- When you need to practice what you preach
- When you want to challenge organizational complacency
- When you want to take your organization to higher levels of performance

There's a certain arrogance you see in some leaders of organizations that are doing pretty well in their markets. They pride themselves on how good their organizations are without ever subjecting them to the rigor of an objective assessment. They take comfort in comparisons against averages rather than world-class benchmarks or even best-in-class.

Some of the leaders who follow in this chapter had some of that initial sense of superiority before they decided to use the Baldrige Criteria for self-assessment or the application process for objective assessment and feedback.

When You Think You're Already a Winner

Terry May, founder and CEO of MESA Products, Inc. (a Baldrige Award small business recipient in 2006 and 2012), described his company as always having high employee satisfaction and customer satisfaction. What the Baldrige journey did for MESA Products, Inc. was enable it to dramatically improve growth and profitability.

How Terry got started on his own journey toward excellence is a funny story that he frequently shares at conferences. He still doesn't know how or why he received his first Baldrige Criteria booklet, but he picked it up while leaving his office on a Friday afternoon thinking it would give him something to read while on jury duty the following Monday. "We'd been on a continuous improvement journey for 10 years, but it wasn't really a journey. It was a series of fixing things. When I first read the Criteria, it was an almost immediate realization that this was the package I had been looking for. We had the beginnings of the individual pieces, but Baldrige wrapped it up so neatly."

Terry was enamored with the Criteria and so confident of the organization's performance that he single-handedly wrote the first application without even telling his other senior leaders. He humorously describes his response to his first feedback report. "First off, I expected to win. Reading my first feedback report was painful, and I got my feelings hurt." This is where, in relaying the story, he starts to grin. "But with the help of a few smart people and some maturing on my part, I got over it and started to understand the value of the feedback."

While the feedback provided by just reviewing an application is valuable, it doesn't compare with the insights that examiners provide after seeing the organization in person on a multiday site visit. After its first application, the organization began to score high enough to earn site visits. It was the additional power of that feedback that helped Terry take his pretty good organization to a higher level of performance. MESA Products won the Baldrige Award in 2006. We were curious about why the company decided to reapply the first year it was eligible in 2012. Terry explained, "Since receiving our first award in 2006, we had doubled in revenue and number of employees. By 2012, only 25 percent of our workforce had been with us in 2006. I felt like during that growth cycle we had relaxed and gotten a little lazy. For me, this was a checkup to see where we were and what we needed to work on. None of us had the expectation we would receive the award the first year we were eligible to come back."

His last comment to us in the interview corroborated what we had hypothesized about pretty good organizations. Terry observed, "The leaders of most companies that are doing okay and are not in crisis don't choose to do something that requires change because that's hard work to become systematic in improvement if there isn't significant motivation to change." (See "Using Crisis to Your Advantage" in Chapter 10.)

David Ramsey, CEO of Charleston Area Medical Center (a 2015 Baldrige Award recipient), first learned about Baldrige not from health care but from its initial targeted sectors—manufacturing and service. He saw it as a measure of excellence for a business to achieve the award. He first began to consider it for his own organization when he heard Sister Mary Jean Ryan speak after SSM Health Care became the first Baldrige Award recipient in health care in 2002.

Dave explained, "Frankly, we had received a number of recognitions for our quality in the early 2000s, and we thought we could find the Baldrige Award to just be another one. We thought we were so good, we'd write an application, the examiners would show up, and 'ta-da.' We didn't know what we didn't know. That's the reason it took 10 years from our first application to receiving the award. By the time we received our first feedback report, we had already figured out we weren't as good as we thought we were. It wasn't going to be as easy as we had thought it would be."

When You Are a Successful Organization with No Burning Platform for Change

Scott McIntyre, managing partner, PricewaterhouseCoopers Public Sector Practice (PwC PSP) (a Baldrige Award service recipient in 2014), wanted to find something that would provide an advantage to differentiate his firm in a very competitive market with low barriers to entry. At an off-site meeting, the partners discussed various options but decided to adopt the Baldrige model for several reasons: (1) It was an established, respected set of Criteria for performance excellence. (2) It gave them the opportunity to gauge their progress, not just against the Criteria but their progress of maturing processes. (3) The value of the objective feedback was compelling.

Scott shared, "We set a goal to win the Baldrige Award by building the processes and creating the culture that would make us worthy of it. Looking back on it, it's really been achieved—that culture of quality." Rick Rodman, partner at PwC PSP, acknowledged the importance of Scott's vision and his championing the effort. "The messaging from Scott was an endorsement of the effort to all of the other partners."

Scott added, "If you know your market really well, you're tempted to think that you know what the customer wants. The Baldrige process forces you to reexamine your assumptions. How do you know that the customer really values this offering or feature of a service? When we redesigned our processes, we began to test options with our customers. In some cases, our clients told us they valued something but not as much as we had thought." One of the advantages of this approach was that the firm was able to detect shifts in client preferences over time, which gave it a competitive advantage.

Another insight for the firm came when the partners realized that, in their industry, supply chain management really is all about getting the best talent through the firm's recruiting, hiring, and onboarding processes. Scott described the challenge in this highly competitive environment, "We can't afford anything less than the best talent. We had to create and maintain a pipeline of talent. We felt we could be faster and could improve the acceptance rate of the most sought-after people in the industry." With the Baldrige framework in mind, they started with a blank sheet of paper and asked themselves what world-class processes would look like.

In its journey to performance excellence, PwC PSP developed a philosophy that simpler was better. Rick shared that this approach included streamlining the strategic planning process from 14 to 4 steps. The partners created greater focus in the organization through integration and alignment that took the key work processes from 10 to 3. Rick explains that these three are "how you win the business, manage the business, and grow your people."

Scott sums it up this way: "Using Baldrige to improve was one of the smartest things we did in our business. It really gave us a touchstone. It really gave us an opportunity to learn about how the Baldrige Criteria and framework could be adapted to our organization . . . and to constantly measure and evaluate ourselves to see how we're doing."

When You Need to Practice What You Preach

The Studer Group is a highly successful consulting firm working with health care organizations. (Since winning the Baldrige Award as a small business recipient in 2010, it has branched out into education, coaching the leaders of school districts.) Sustainability (the long-term viability of a business) has always been important in health care and has grown increasingly challenging. Quint Studer, founder of the Studer Group, got exposed to the Baldrige Criteria around 2000. He could see how the framework would complement the principles and practices the firm was already teaching its clients and would reinforce a focus on measurement and outcomes.

The Studer Group consultants started asking their clients, "Have you looked at Baldrige?" As Quint says, "All of a sudden, our clients start winning the Baldrige Award. Then it became a credibility issue for us. It's easier to tell someone else to embark on this journey than to do it ourselves. We told our employees that we weren't out to win the award, but we were out to improve our processes, benchmark against world-class performance, and then sustain our gains." Quint also shared, "It's pretty simple to be motivated to change when you're losing money. The danger is when you're doing okay" [and tackling change doesn't seem so urgent]. This same sentiment has been shared by other senior leaders and is echoed in the following sections.

When You Want to Challenge Organizational Complacency

John Kotter, in his 1996 book *Leading Change*, said the biggest enemy to change is complacency—"becoming satisfied with our current results and unaware of how the known and predictable erode performance." He emphasized this point again in a *Harvard Business Review* article in 2007, even citing organizations where the senior leaders "manufactured a crisis" to instill a sense of urgency.[1]

Dr. David Spong is the retired leader of two different Boeing divisions to receive the Baldrige Award (Boeing Mobility, formerly Airlift & Tanker [A&T], in the manufacturing category in 1998 and Boeing Support Systems, formerly Aerospace Support, in the service category in 2003). He is also, to date, the only person to lead organizations in two different categories to win the Baldrige Award.

Unlike A&T, which was in crisis when it began the Baldrige journey, Boeing Support Systems was a relatively good organization with good results. The organization's leaders felt that continuing along the same path was fine. However, David used the approach cited by John Kotter and created some constructive "tension" around the need for change based on the previous year, when the division had overpromised and under-delivered to both its customers and the corporation. David reports, "I declared, 'We are going to embark on a Baldrige journey,' and then I started down the road with whoever would follow." A few of the senior leaders rapidly got on board, but others dragged their feet.

David began holding a "Baldrige off-site" every three months. The vice presidents who had been named Category Champions had to stand up in front of the group and report the progress in their categories. External consultants were present who were asked to validate the Champions' assessment of progress, and they were not reluctant to point out if such progress was overstated. As David said, "VPs do not like to be embarrassed in front of their peers and the rest of the organization." Once these executives realized they were being held accountable, "they also realized they had to lead and actually demonstrate improved processes and results." David shared that when the VPs saw that they were generating and sustaining improved results, they became true believers.

When You Want to Take Your Organization to Higher Levels of Performance

Many of the leaders we interviewed talked about setting aggressive targets. Matt Fleming, president of MidwayUSA (a 2009 and 2015 Baldrige Award recipient), recently said at a conference that for every metric, he wants to see the goal. "If a measurement doesn't have a goal, it's just trivia to me." He also wants to know how the goal was set. "We insist on having bold goals because that's in keeping with our vision—'to be the best run, most respected business in America, for the benefit of our Customers.'"

For AtlantiCare (a 2009 Baldrige Award recipient in health care), it's about shooting for top decile performance in all of its key measures—and not just clinical indicators—customer and employee engagement, as well. At the Baldrige Quest for Excellence® Conference following AtlantiCare's win, CEO David Tilton talked about becoming "award worthy." We asked him what that meant. David explained, "I heard people who were the doubters, the cynics. They thought this was all about winning the crystal. They thought it was about me standing up on a stage accepting the award. I knew that to be worthy of this award really spoke to our mission. And if we can be performing at a very high level, we're achieving our mission. That's what 'award worthy' meant to me."

Diane Brockmeier, CEO of Mid-America Transplant Services (a 2015 Baldrige Award recipient), said, "We had long been a data-driven organization, but without comparative data, you quickly believe your own propaganda that you're doing really well. Baldrige taught us the value of benchmarking against others." When the company originally started on its journey, there was no publicly available data regarding the organ donor and transplant industry. It led the initiative to lobby its industry association to collect data that could be used to establish the benchmark performance across a variety of transplant-specific measures.

Dr. JoAnn Sternke, superintendent of the Pewaukee School District (a Baldrige Award recipient in 2013), deliberately chooses to compare her school district with a group of high-achieving school districts across the state of Wisconsin rather than against the averages of all school districts. This keeps the organization focused on excellence.

> ### When You're Already a Pretty Good Organization—Checklist
>
> 1. If you think your organization is already high performing, how do you know?
> 2. What are the comparisons that you use to evaluate the quality of your results—averages, top quartile or top decile, best-in-class benchmarks, or world-class benchmarks?
> 3. How do you get objective feedback about all facets of your organization?
> 4. If you're in a highly competitive market, how do you differentiate yourself with quality?
> 5. If you face organizational complacency, how could you create some constructive "tension" to challenge it?

Maintaining Momentum
When Facing a Downturn

- What if the prospect is going out of business?
- What if the downturn is precipitous?
- What if you encounter "the perfect storm"?
- What if confidence is shaken in your whole industry?
- What if you have a challenging business model?
- Creating an "all-weather" organization

Employees' expectations for leaders increase during a crisis. They expect more communication, more real information, more reassurances, and more empathy. During an economic downturn or industry shakeup, many employees become anxious about the potential loss of jobs—especially their own. As Keith McFarland says in his book *The Breakthrough Company*, "Everyone lives each day on the edge, and rumors fly around the water cooler and the coffee room. When [senior leaders] cut off the flow of information to the [employees] in difficult times, you leave them to develop their own negative fantasies about what's happening, and they often dream up doomsday scenarios that are far worse than the reality."[1] And since the employees aren't running the show, they look to the leaders to demonstrate a commitment to the vision, to the organization, and to them.

Kay was a senior leader in Arizona for an aerospace corporation going through enormous upheaval with mergers, acquisitions, divestitures, and restructuring at the same time as defense spending budgets were being cut drastically. In her last position with that organization, the business unit had four different presidents in only 13 months, with the last one serving as an "acting president." Trying to keep employees focused and productive during those times was nearly impossible. In fact, one of her colleagues told her that each day he came in to work, he was "just trying not to spook the herd."

In times like these, leadership becomes more crucial. Your best employees, your top performers, are likely to jump ship for a better opportunity unless they are convinced that the senior leaders have the conviction and the competence to address and overcome the situation. This is also an opportunity for senior leaders to tap into the creativity and innovation in the workforce by asking for their help in identifying ideas that can address some of the challenges to sustain the organization during the crisis. Ken Schnitzer from Park Place Dealerships gave an example of this in Chapter 5.

What we have seen other exemplary leaders in these situations do—and have done ourselves—is to volunteer first to make sacrifices. For example, if salaries are going to be frozen, or worse yet, cut, senior leaders ought to be the first to cut theirs and by a larger proportion than the rest of the workforce. And this is not the time to be humble about these actions. Without communication that "we are all in this together," employees are likely to see senior leaders as immune to any of the hardships they are facing.

These are also the times when employees test the senior leaders' commitments to the organization's stated values.

Despite the stress, tension, and ambiguity of a crisis, do the senior leaders still treat employees with respect? If integrity is one of the organization's values, do employees observe senior leaders behaving and communicating with transparency? Jim Collins says, "Great organizations keep clear the difference between their core values (which never change) and operating strategies and cultural practices (which endlessly adapt to a changing world)."[2]

Finally, as we stated in the previous chapter, sometimes a crisis can be put to good use to shake up a complacent culture. A crisis may offer a senior leader just the opportunity to execute other planned actions with a greater sense of urgency to accelerate their implementation.

What if the Prospect Is Going Out of Business?

This is a potential crisis of huge proportions. Depending on the issues and how long the leader has to address them, it might be too late. And what if this potential crisis is not entirely in the hands of the senior leader?

That was the situation faced by the U.S. Army Armament Research, Development and Engineering Center (ARDEC) (a Baldrige Award government recipient in 2007) in 1995. Joe Brescia, director for strategic management and process improvement, described its close call with a DoD base realignment and closure (BRAC): "It was a major wake-up call for those of us at ARDEC at the time. Our commanding general, General James Boddie, became convinced that the organization needed to radically change its approach and operate 'more like a for-profit business.' That meant finding new and innovative ways to exceed customer expectations with respect to cost, schedule, and performance. After researching several quality management models and consulting with leaders throughout DoD and industry, he became convinced that the Baldrige framework represented the best course of action to manage ARDEC's business." And to keep it in business.

In addition, the Baldrige journey appealed to the culture of the organization because of its lack of prescriptiveness. "ARDEC has highly intelligent people who can find many ways to attack a problem. The Baldrige framework allowed us to leverage that during these challenging times," said Joe.

ARDEC conducts periodic external assessments and actively benchmarks with other organizations to maintain the momentum of transformational change. By providing a "second set of eyes," external assessments and benchmarking serve as excellent venues to validate and share what they are doing right as well as to help identify potential areas for improvement. This has become so embedded in the ARDEC culture that the organization has benchmarked over 20 different government agencies since 2007, including the VA Cooperative Studies Program (a 2009 Baldrige Award government recipient).

What if the Downturn Is Precipitous?

Sometimes even well-run organizations find themselves facing a crisis not of their own making. That was the situation that Paul Worstell, retired CEO of PRO-TEC Coating Company (a Baldrige Award small business recipient in 2007), faced. He was presented with the award (made of beautiful Steuben crystal) in April 2008. The company was operating at 115 percent equipment utilization. It had a solid track record of outstanding profitability with greater than 30 percent profit sharing for the associates. The organization was developing new products, and safety performance was at world-class levels. "We were flying!" exclaimed Paul. "In the summer of 2008, we had an opportunity to expand our business with a third production line."

And then came September 2008 with the near collapse of the automotive industry, the company's sole customer base. Utilization dropped overnight to less than 40 percent. "Our first instinct was to panic, but we said, 'No, let's do what made us successful—do Baldrige.' However, we would be applying it in a very, very different environment."

Throughout their journey to performance excellence, Paul and his senior leaders had developed a culture of continuous improvement by involving the entire workforce in projects. Once again, they appealed to the workforce for their help in meeting the challenge of the downturn. They came up with hundreds of ideas to reduce costs. The company eliminated all outsourcing. "Guys who had been working on the production line took over security, grounds keeping, etc. We took over housekeeping. In fact, as president, my job was to clean the men's restroom on the second floor of administration." This is an example of what we described earlier about the senior leaders being visible in making personal sacrifices during a crisis.

The company operated in these austere ways for more than eight months. There had never been a layoff at PRO-TEC Coating Company, and there wasn't one during this time. Even more impressive, the company remained profitable during the crisis.

What if You Encounter "the Perfect Storm"?

Sometimes in business, as in Sebastian Junger's book of the same name, you encounter a perfect storm—an unlikely combination of events that can have disastrous consequences. Jordan Case, president of Park Place Lexus (a Baldrige Award small business recipient in 2005), described the "perfect storm" that hit his organization in 2008–2009. On top of the severe economic recession that certainly was impacting the sale of luxury automobiles, the dealership was dealt a blow to its inventory when Japan suffered a series of earthquakes that impacted its production capabilities. For example, the store in Plano went from having 400 to 500 cars available to having about 60 on the lot.

Based on typical models of compensation for sales consultants, these employees would have had a dramatic reduction in their normal earnings. Earlier in this chapter we talked about the potential exodus of high-performing employees during a crisis. Such deep cuts to previously earned income could have been just the trigger for the best sales consultants to leave. However, Park Place Lexus made the decision to pay its sales consultants based on their prior year's average earnings until the inventory began to be restored. Jordan said, "We didn't lose any of our salespeople. Everything actually turned out pretty good. It would have been far more expensive to replace the sales force when you consider the costs of recruiting and training, and the lost sales while new people got up to speed."

Because of its ongoing commitment to managing the business using the Baldrige framework, Park Place Lexus weathered this "perfect storm" and demonstrated its core conviction of "Unwavering Integrity: We build trust with our members and clients through honesty and respect. We do what we say—we honor our commitments."

What if Confidence Is Shaken in Your Whole Industry?

Sometimes the problem isn't distrust of a single organization but a massive lack of confidence in an entire industry—in this case, the financial industry. That was the scenario in 2008 with another "perfect storm" when the American housing market crumbled in the wake of failed mortgage companies, the associated collapse of several major investment banks, and the near bankruptcy of several large insurance companies.

Gerry Agnes stepped into the role of CEO at Elevations Credit Union (a Baldrige Award nonprofit recipient in 2014) only a few months before that financial crisis in September 2008. With the board's endorsement, he had already launched the journey to win the Baldrige Award as a BHAG (Big Hairy Audacious Goal). When the financial crisis hit, several of his senior leaders questioned, "Are you sure you want to do this (Baldrige) now?" Other people asked why he would spend financial capital and human resources in the midst of this crisis to adopt the Baldrige framework. Gerry responded, "We thought to ourselves, we're really at a fork in the road. If we take the wrong fork, we might end up in mediocrity. We wanted to make sure we understood who we are, where we're going, and how we're going to get there."[3]

He used the time during this serious recession to focus the organization around the mission, vision, and values. He also described "setting up a framework for any organization to prosper in any economic environment." Prior to the recession, the organization had done very well with a good brand in the community and good market penetration. However, the Credit Union had not put systematic processes and a robust measurement system in place. Implementing the Baldrige framework created an environment where the entire organization was engaged in Business Process Management (BPM). (See Appendix A for a link to Elevation Credit Union's BPM workbook.)

Peter Raymond, partner at PricewaterhouseCoopers Public Sector Practice (PwC PSP) (a Baldrige Award service recipient in 2014), described the response his firm had in the face of a government shutdown in October 2013. "We had addressed this as a possible scenario in our Strategic Planning Process. When the shutdown became more likely, we started messaging with our staff 15 days in advance. When the shutdown became a reality, our competitors laid off people. We didn't. Some of our people spent the time completing mandatory training. Some were moved to other (nongovernment) projects. Still others were focused on internal process improvement. The bottom line: we were more profitable at the end of the year than we had anticipated." By not laying people off, PwC PSP actually deployed some of them to address opportunities for improvement that had been identified in feedback received during its Baldrige journey.

What if You Have a Challenging Business Model?

Anyone who follows the news about the health care industry knows how organizations have been negatively impacted by changing reimbursements. In fact, an article published on January 25, 2016, by the blog *Becker's Hospital Review* listed 10 hospitals that had filed for bankruptcy protection or closed just since December 2015.[4] In that kind of environment, it might be tempting for health care executives to view taking on a Baldrige journey as too costly, too time-consuming in the midst of financial firefighting.

That's the opposite of what the senior leaders at Charleston Area Medical Center (CAMC) (a 2015 Baldrige Award recipient) believed. Many of its patients can't cover the costs of their medical care. The only way for the organization to survive is by engaging its employees in process improvement that generates cost savings and increases productivity and efficiency.

CAMC found that using the Baldrige Criteria was synergistic with its use of Lean, which it calls "Transforming Care Together," or TCT. Brenda Grant, chief strategy officer, said "The feedback we got from our early applications helped us to prioritize, and the goal cascade process we developed helped to align the improvements we were making." Dr. Glenn Crotty, COO, followed up, "TCT is our form of the Toyota lean production system. Combining that with the Baldrige framework, which is so process- and systems-driven, just became the way of life at CAMC. And as people could see how it made their jobs easier, the momentum grew. For instance, reducing the time to complete forms on the nursing unit from four hours to 50 minutes gets people excited about what else could be improved." The organization also had developed internal expertise in Six Sigma in 2000 with six Black Belts. David Ramsey, CEO of CAMC, described that the organization first had to figure out how to use these folks and their capabilities. He said, "They were the data and improvement experts who could help the departments identify projects, collect the data, graph it in a way that people could understand, and—importantly—hold the gains."

When asked about how extensive CAMC's use of technology was to its success, Dave laughed. "Our 'technology' is just computers and a statistical program that helps us analyze and graph the data. Six Sigma expertise was our technology that helped us diagnose processes." Brenda added, "As we have seen increases in employee engagement, we've also been able to achieve impressive results. Over the last 15 years, we've taken $177 million out of our budget, and last year it was $21 million." CAMC's board takes a longer-term view and bases incentive compensation on two factors: financial performance and goal attainment. David said, "Even if we have a bad year for our financials, the board has chosen to reward for the goals attained."

Creating an "All-Weather" Organization

Some of the leaders described their desire to create an organization that could ride whatever economic condition it faces. Harry Zechman, COO, and Rob Ecklin, president, of Stoner, Inc. (a Baldrige Award small business recipient in 2003), described their ability to deliver consistent results over the past 12 years, including a major recession. They described building an engaged workforce along the journey that is reflected by very little employee turnover. Harry says, "Because of the Baldrige Award, we got put on the radar screen—in a good way, especially for a small company. We're at the point now where we have young people who are coming from good universities in our area who are seeking us out for employment." The robust processes they developed along the way also have enabled the organization to adapt to changes in the economic and competitive environment. Harry and Rob credit their Baldrige journey for developing an "all-weather" organization.

Several other leaders of Baldrige Award recipients cited their ability to maintain momentum during a downturn because of a robust strategic planning process. "It keeps an organization focused on long-term gains and prevents knee-jerk reactions to short-term pains," explained Ken Schiller, co-owner and cofounder of K&N Management, a 2010 Baldrige Award small business recipient.

Ken Schnitzer, chairman of Park Place Dealerships (the parent organization of Park Place Lexus, a 2005 Baldrige Award recipient), agrees about the importance of a good strategic planning process, but his lesson during the organization's Baldrige journey was related to a word defined in the Glossary of the Baldrige Excellence Framework, *key*. Ken said, "Our strategic plan before we started using Baldrige had about eight objectives. We didn't have any focus, so we didn't get any of them done." That same focus is often described by Dr. JoAnn Sternke, superintendent of the Pewaukee School District (a 2013 Baldrige Award recipient). She says, "You can have all the 'purpose' (vision) in your heart, but without the ability to execute your strategic plan with fidelity, it's just good intentions."

Dr. Mike Sather, former director of the Veterans Affairs Cooperative Studies Program Clinical Research Pharmacy Coordinating Center (a Baldrige Award government recipient in 2009), stated, "Many organizations believe they have a good bottom line, and they don't need Baldrige. We believe Baldrige is the most holistic approach to managing an organization and contributing to your sustainability in good times and in bad times."

Tommy Gonzalez, former city manager for the City of Irving (a Baldrige Award government recipient in 2012), described how putting things in place to support people in doing their jobs and taking away obstacles convinced his organization that the Baldrige journey was working. Employees were trained and engaged in the use of Lean Six Sigma to improve processes, reduce inefficiencies, and generate cost savings. When the economy hit the downturn, the City of Irving decreased its workforce by 10 percent through attrition, yet it gave incentives and raises and promoted more than 600 people. In fact, during that same challenging time period, it was the only city in North Texas to receive a Best Places to Work award.

Facing a downturn can be a scary time for any leader without the ability to predict how deep and how long the challenging situation will be. However, leaders who remain consistent with many of the core concepts of the Baldrige Excellence Framework (described in Chapter 1) provide a sense of stability to their employees during difficult times. These include valuing people, organizational learning and agility, and focus on success. The leaders interviewed for this chapter demonstrated these and helped their organizations emerge even stronger from an economic downturn.

Maintaining Momentum When Facing a Downturn—Checklist

1. How do your employees know how well—or how poorly— your organization is doing in the market?
2. What would you tell your workforce if your organization risked going out of business? How would you engage them in overcoming the challenges?
3. What alternatives could you create to laying off employees during a downturn?
4. What approaches do you need to take to create an "all-weather" organization?

The Challenges of Being a Very Large Organization

- Cutting through the bureaucracy to connect with employees
- Creating alignment in a very large organization
- When your large organization is geographically dispersed
- Using a crisis to challenge the inertia of a large organization
- Being a pocket of excellence in a very large organization

Anyone who has ever worked for a very large organization can tell you there are benefits to it, but there are also challenges. Both of us have worked for and with very large organizations, so we have firsthand knowledge about these challenges. Some of them include the increased complexity, particularly with cross-functional processes and their handoffs. Another is often the slow pace at which decisions get made as the requests go up the chain of command and the responses come back down again. And people can feel like very little fish in a very big pond, unable to relate how their day-to-day work is connected to anything larger than themselves.

There are also, of course, challenges for the leaders of very large organizations. The message they are trying to communicate often gets garbled or lost in an organizational equivalent of the old game of "telephone." Maintaining alignment of objectives and measures can be difficult through multiple layers and further complicated with different geographical locations. Decisions about what should be centralized versus decentralized fall to the senior leaders in large organizations along with what processes should be standardized versus those that should be tailored to meet local needs and preferences.

The leaders of some very large organizations that have won the Baldrige Award share some of their insights and strategies in the following sections.

Cutting Through the Bureaucracy to Connect with Employees

Dr. David Spong is the retired leader of two different Boeing divisions to receive the Baldrige Award (Boeing Mobility—formerly Airlift & Tanker [A&T] in the manufacturing category in 1998 and Boeing Support Systems—formerly Aerospace Support in the service category in 2003). And, as we mentioned in Chapter 6, he is also, to date, the only person to lead organizations in two different categories to win the Baldrige Award. David acknowledges some of the difficulties he faced and how he addressed them.

The Boeing divisions he led were large, layered organizations. For consistency in messaging, David would create a kind of "State of the Union" presentation for the senior leaders at the division's headquarters. The presentation was then deployed to all of the site leaders. He made it a requirement for the site leaders to meet with their employees using the same set of slides. The site leaders could augment the slide deck with site-specific information, but they could not alter or delete any slides from the master presentation.

Other ways that David dealt with the frequent challenge of frontline staff having access to senior leaders were through a true open door policy (see Chapter 11 for an example of this in action) and a system called Dialogue with David. Through that system, employees were encouraged to e-mail him with any questions or concerns. Many times, he would pick up the phone in response to an e-mail and talk directly with the (very surprised) employee. This is one example of leveraging an organization's "grapevine" to a senior leader's advantage. The employees receiving David's calls would quickly spread the word to their coworkers. In fairly short order, it became common knowledge that David was approachable, that he listened, and that he was a straight shooter when it came to responding.

Creating Alignment in a Very Large Organization

In Chapter 4 we described approaches that other Baldrige Award winning organizations used to create alignment in their organizations by developing a line of sight between every employee and the top-level objectives. David also used this approach to align the organization by establishing a few critical objectives at the top. These objectives and their requirements were flowed down throughout the organization, and the required actions and associated metrics flowed back up. This ensured that employees saw how their day-to-day work contributed to the overall success of the organization.

David used a second approach to create alignment in the organizational structure he built. Initially, he received a lot of criticism because of the large number of direct reports he had (about 25). He was told that no one can manage more than 10 people. He responded, "I'm not trying to manage them; I'm trying to lead them!" He also felt that it was important that no function be subordinated under another function. He felt that all of his senior leaders deserved a place at the table.

His organizational chart was an interesting matrix with the senior leader (him) at the top and the senior leaders with profit and loss responsibility in the center. On the left-hand side were all of the sites, and on the right-hand side were all of the functions. Execution was accomplished vertically, while integration occurred horizontally. Each box on the organization chart had defined, explicit RAAs—Responsibility, Authority, and Accountability. David says, "The problem in a lot of organizations that don't work is that people are given responsibility and accountability, but they don't have the authority they need to make things happen."

The third approach was a change in the way that incentive compensation was determined. For the first time, David brought all of his senior leaders together to discuss who should receive incentive bonuses and at what percent based on the collective view of how well an employee was supporting the performance excellence journey in line with the expectations along with how well employees had accomplished their individual goals and objectives. David is not sure how, but this new approach also hit the "grapevine" and reinforced the belief that this journey was indeed something to which the senior leaders were committed.

The fourth approach that David used to align the organization was the development of the Rules of Conduct. These were developed by the senior leaders at an off-site meeting early on the journey. David admitted, "It was painful as hell at first. We spent almost the whole first day debating and wordsmithing. When we broke for the day, I was afraid we were going to spend the second day in the same mode. Miraculously, when we reconvened, everyone said they were 'good to go' with the rules we had drafted the first day. What made the Rules of Conduct so powerful was that we, as senior leaders, called each other on any violations. That sent a strong message to the rest of the organization well beyond any posters on the walls or badge extenders."

When Your Large Organization Is Geographically Dispersed

The challenge for David Spong with taking the Boeing Support Systems division on the Baldrige journey was that it was a very large organization with more than 13,000 employees spread across eight major sites in six states. To apply for the Baldrige Award as a single division, he needed each site to begin its own journey to performance excellence. This was key to creating a common language and ensuring that each site and site leader were at a similar maturity in the process. He challenged the site leaders to begin applying for their state program's highest level award. When each site had finally earned the highest level award, David said, "That integrated the whole organization."

What he hadn't anticipated was the value of people having a single framework with which to run the business. David's boss used to take the corporate jet to visit various sites. He commented once to David that there was something different about David's sites, "It's amazing that when I visit your sites, everyone seems to know what's going on and speak the same language."

Another David, David Ramsey, CEO of Charleston Area Medical Center (a 2015 Baldrige Award recipient), described the challenges of keeping everyone on the same page with three hospitals in about a 30-mile radius. "When we started on the journey about 10 years ago, we kept getting feedback from the employees saying that they didn't know what was going on. So, we do rounding. We created 'Inside the Board Room' to share what happened at the recent board meeting with all employees. Each hospital has a newsletter that has information about the system as well as information tailored for that audience. Frankly, one of the best things we do is the Manager Forum, where any manager can attend any forum at any location. That gives them the opportunity to see what's happening at another hospital."

Dr. Rulon Stacey, former CEO of Poudre Valley Health System (a 2008 Baldrige Award health care recipient), describes the additional difficulty of standardizing performance in an organization that has several locations. "It's hard to get past the geography and the cultural differences of how the organizations developed—this is particularly true with mergers and acquisitions. That's why using the Baldrige Criteria is so important in large organizations. It's the only hope for creating alignment."

Using a Crisis to Challenge the Inertia of a Large Organization

Joe Brescia, director of strategic management and process improvement of the U.S. Army Armament Research, Development and Engineering Center (ARDEC) (a Baldrige Award government recipient in 2007), observes that it often takes a crisis to convince large organizations that change is required. "In ARDEC's case, the organization had survived a close call with a DoD base realignment and closure (BRAC) back in 1995. ARDEC's commanding general at the time, General James Boddie, became convinced that the organization needed to radically change its approach and operate 'more like a for-profit business.' This meant finding new and innovative ways to exceed ARDEC's customer expectations with respect to cost, schedule, and performance to better serve the interests and needs of 'Our Ultimate Customer'—the U.S. Soldier."

That said, short of an actual crisis to create the necessary burning platform, it can be very difficult to make the case for a wholesale change. In very large organizations, both public and private, there can often be a lot of inertia to resist change, especially if things are perceived to be going well. According to Joe, "That's where visionary leadership comes in—it must both inspire and galvanize the entire organization for action. Once the course of action is decided, leaders must exercise great perseverance. After all, you can't expect to turn a battleship around on a dime. But by making a series of small, gradual improvements over time, and celebrating the wins as you go, you can eventually make some rather significant course changes."

Being a Pocket of Excellence in a Very Large Organization

The Veterans Affairs Cooperative Studies Program Clinical Research Pharmacy Coordinating Center (VACSP) was a Baldrige Award government recipient in 2009. Although VACSP had only 112 employees at that time, the Department of Veterans Affairs had 297,000 employees in 2009. With that size comes a lot of oversight, a lot of regulations, and a lot of bureaucracy.

Dr. Mike Sather, former director of VACSP, says, "We were told to run the organization like a business. However, as part of a government entity, many of the employees don't know what it's like to run a business. A lot of the regulations don't help you to run your organization like a business." They looked to outside organizations for best practices they could implement.

In the course of applying to its state program, Quality New Mexico, the VA's Baldrige-based program (the former Carey Award program), and Baldrige, VACSP hosted 12 site visits. Mike says, "One of our most gratifying times during the multiple site visits was having the examiners say, 'I can't believe this is a government organization.' And 'This is the VA's best-kept secret.'"

We've worked in and worked with some extremely large organizations, and the challenges of effective communication are exponentially greater than in their smaller counterparts. What makes the Baldrige Excellence Framework so powerful is its ability to align tens of thousands of employees dispersed not only across the country but internationally with the most important objectives of the organization. The framework also emphasizes the need for organizational agility that challenges the bureaucracy often seen in very large organizations. These two attributes contribute to developing a formidable advantage over competitors.

The Challenges of Being a Very Large Organization—Checklist

1. How bureaucratic is your organization? Do departments or functions operate in silos? How do you know?
2. How do you make yourself and your senior leaders accessible to employees?
3. How do you create alignment through multiple layers and across locations?
4. Would it be helpful to "create" a crisis to challenge the inertia in your organization?
5. What communication methods could improve the information flow with employees?

9

The Challenges of Being a Very Small Organization

- Typical excuses why small organizations can't embark on a Baldrige journey
- How formalizing processes helps small organizations
- Why prioritization is key
- The upside to being a small organization

According to the sector definitions for Baldrige, a small business has 500 or fewer paid employees. However, since the Baldrige Program began keeping these statistics (in 2004), the smallest Baldrige Award recipient has been Texas Nameplate, which had 43 employees when it won its second award in 2004. That's fewer employees than there are pages in a Baldrige application!

Small organizations struggle with being able to provide career development opportunities for employees seeking upward mobility. Absent those opportunities, small organizations must find creative ways to motivate and retain their workforce. Also in small organizations, and especially those under 100 employees, there are going to be issues around resources—not just financial but the human kind. The challenge of embarking on the Baldrige journey as a very small business is that no one is a specialist. Everyone wears multiple hats. Supporting site visits while continuing to operate also puts a lot stress on the organization. Something like going on a performance excellence journey can seem like an impossible undertaking.

In addition, most small organizations do not have any internal experts to help them understand the Baldrige Excellence Framework or the in-house capabilities of writing and publishing an application. If large organizations flinch from the challenge, it's almost easy to let small organizations off the hook.

Typical Excuses Why Small Organizations Can't Embark on a Baldrige Journey

Terry May, CEO of MESA Products, Inc. (a Baldrige Award small business recipient in 2006 and 2012), says, "*Using* the framework isn't a challenge in a small organization, but putting together an application is very difficult for most small organizations. We didn't have any experts in the Baldrige Criteria, didn't have any money, and didn't have any professional writers. However, using the framework is almost easier in a small organization." He describes how putting the application together became less difficult over time. "It took a lot of energy, but you start to realize this process of submitting an application and getting feedback is making a difference, and your attitude changes."

However, Terry is quick to point out that even small organizations can face one of the same challenges that large organizations do. "Our biggest challenge now is communication because we are scattered across the region and now multiple states."

Quint Studer, founder of the Studer Group (a Baldrige Award small business recipient in 2010), described the challenge for his organization and other small businesses in embarking on a Baldrige journey. "It's a psychological thing. You rationalize that we'll wait until we're bigger. First, we'll put in an evaluation system and job descriptions. Then, we'll do a strategic plan. Then, we'll do something else. You'll never get there." Quint attributes embarking on the Baldrige journey as a forcing function to implement these changes that many small businesses frequently find excuses for not doing.

Many small organizations say that they can't find the comparative data they need to assess their progress and demonstrate good performance in their applications. And that may be partly true because they don't have dedicated data analysts or the skills to research those benchmarks. We have found the following things to be helpful to small organizations in finding comparative data:

- Attend Baldrige-related conferences and network with attendees and presenters.
- Review relevant Baldrige Award applications posted on the Baldrige website.
- Reach out to industry associations.
- If you are in a regulated industry, identify what measures are required to be reported—those are likely to be publicly available and found through an Internet search.

How Formalizing Processes Helps Small Organizations

Some small organizations are busy being busy. They can't imagine making time to develop and implement systematic processes. Yet it is that very discipline that allows organizations—of all sizes—to get out of a mode of constant firefighting. Ken Schiller, co-owner and cofounder of K&N

Management (a 2010 small business Baldrige Award recipient), sums it up nicely, "Before starting our Baldrige journey, we were working our butts off. We didn't know how we were doing, probably above average. Efforts were in different directions. Baldrige brought us into alignment. It is a tool to channel your efforts. We all started rowing in the same direction. Baldrige is the key to winning results and world-class excellence."[1]

Maryruth Butler, executive director of Kindred Nursing and Rehabilitation—Mountain Valley (a 2011 Gold Award recipient for the AHCA/NCAL Quality Award Program), said, "Being on this journey changed our culture. Originally, we achieved good results because we were lucky. We didn't have systematic, repeatable processes to address problems. We went from being very reactive to being proactive. We put leading indicators in place. Rarely do we have surprises anymore. We can predict what is going to happen and change our actions if necessary."

Why Prioritization Is Key

As we stated before, small organizations have limited resources, especially when it comes to the people part of any equation. While large organizations can tackle multiple initiatives simultaneously, their much smaller counterparts must prioritize and focus on what is most important to accomplish.

Paul Worstell, retired CEO of PRO-TEC Coating Company, (a Baldrige Award small business recipient in 2007), describes his organization's previous approach. "We were running our business very traditionally. Come in each day. Identify the crisis of the day. Fight fires. Go home at the end of a very long day. Repeat."

The organization also operates in a highly regulated environment. It began in the late 1990s with its automotive customers requiring their suppliers to be certified to ISO 9000. Then, it was required to become certified to ISO 14000, the environmental standard. It faced strict OSHA requirements. Preparing for all of the associated audits was challenging for the small company. "We said that we wanted to find a quality management system that allowed us to be ISO-compliant every day." The challenge with being a small organization is that you can't do it all—you simply don't have the resources. Prioritization becomes key. When PRO-TEC Coating Company received its first feedback report, Paul says that the leaders realized that they "had to get clarity on where our gaps were and prioritize the things that we were going to build processes around and then fully deploy them."

Although Pewaukee School District won the Baldrige Award in 2013 in the education category, with 296 employees it could easily be classified as a small organization. Dr. JoAnn Sternke, superintendent, says that prioritization was also key for the school district. When the leaders leveraged their feedback reports, they asked, "What should we celebrate? What should we consciously decide *not* to undertake—at least not now? We elected to put only one or two big items in place [in any given year]."

The Upside to Being a Small Organization

While large organizations may struggle with having consistency in communication and standardizing processes, this may be one area where small organizations have an advantage. The senior leaders often know each of their employees—by name, their interests, their families, even their pets! In high-performing small organizations, employees typically describe their colleagues as their "work families." And communication doesn't suffer from the filtering and distortion that comes with going through multiple layers.

In 2003 when Stoner, Inc. won the Baldrige Award, it had fewer than 50 employees. However, Harry Zechman, COO, and Rob Ecklin, president, acknowledged that being small did have some advantages. "It's quicker on the 'sell' side. You get more and broader involvement and support because you have to."

The Challenges of Being a Very Small Organization—Checklist

1. How could making the systems and processes of the Baldrige framework more robust help your organization and position it for growth?
2. What are some of the ways that you could develop internal expertise? (See Chapter 14.)
3. Where could you find other resources that could help you on your journey? (See Appendix A.)
4. How do you prioritize all of the various things your organization *could* do to the vital few to provide focus?
5. What is keeping you from getting started on the journey to performance excellence?

Getting All of the Senior Leaders on Board

- How you frame it makes a difference
- When your senior leaders are supportive but don't know how to get started
- Getting nonemployed physicians on board in a health care system
- When you face skepticism
- When you face open resistance
- When you face passive-aggressive resistance
- Using crisis to your advantage
- When you encounter early disappointment

We're of the opinion after working with many, many organizations on their journeys that the transformational change won't be successful or sustainable unless the senior leaders have bought in. This belief is underscored by the research that Jim Collins and his team did for *Good to Great*. "In fact, leaders of companies that go from good to great start not with 'where' but with 'who.' They start by getting the right people on the bus, the wrong people off the bus, and the right people in the right seats."[1]

While Jim Collins was talking about "right" in terms of "A-level people who are willing to put out A-plus effort," he also meant having senior leaders who wanted to be on the bus and were committed to the journey.

The leaders we interviewed all echoed this sentiment in one way or another. Some exhibited more patience than others in waiting for their senior leaders to buy in to the journey to performance excellence, but none tolerated blockers of the change or even passive resistance for very long.

One sentiment that we heard from several leaders was that how the journey is announced is key to warding off resistance. Their experiences are described in the following section.

How You Frame It Makes a Difference

Quint Studer, founder of the Studer Group (a Baldrige Award small business recipient in 2010), says that none of his senior leaders resisted undertaking the Baldrige journey but he sees it in some of his clients' organizations. "It's how you explain it and frame it. You don't say that you're out to win the award. We're here to improve our processes, to benchmark, and to sustain the gains. People are so busy that it can't be about the award. Tie it back to what's important to the organization."

Paul Worstell, retired CEO of PRO-TEC Coating Company (a Baldrige Award small business recipient in 2007), believes the most important role of the senior leader is to make it clear the decision to go on the Baldrige journey has been made. "You can acknowledge that it isn't going to be easy, but this bus has left the station. This isn't additional work; we are going to change the way we do our work. It's the way we're going to run our business."

In a similar vein, David Tilton, CEO of AtlantiCare (a Baldrige Award health care recipient in 2009), had made quality a priority at the organization. Beginning initially with a focus on regulatory compliance, then achieving Magnet status (an award given by the American Nurses Credentialing Center [ANCC], an affiliate of the American Nurses Association, to hospitals that satisfy a set of criteria designed to measure the strength and quality of their nursing), and then more rigorous standards, the Baldrige Criteria was a natural progression. "When we made the decision to pursue Baldrige, we had no thought about going for an award. We saw it as a framework to improve the leadership skills of the senior leadership team." Joan Brennan, VP of quality and performance, continued, "We agreed the senior leaders would have to learn it, teach it, and work with it on category teams. Then the senior leaders were expected to identify our gaps and issues." David had just been named the system's CEO in 2007. When they received their first feedback report from the national program, one of the senior leaders said, "I'm glad we're done with that, and we can move on to something else." David replied, "We're just starting."

The senior leaders at K&N Management (a Baldrige Award small business recipient in 2010) had been exposed to Baldrige for many years through their benchmarking of Pal's Sudden Service, the first fast-food chain to ever win the Baldrige Award (2001). Once they decided to adopt the Criteria and begin the process of submitting applications, all of K&N Management's senior leaders were on board for the Baldrige journey. However, says Ken Schiller, co-owner and cofounder, "Some of the management at the stores weren't. They didn't see the need for change because 'Business is good. We're making money.'" The K&N senior leaders knew it was important to get these store managers on board, so they worked with them to help them see how this journey aligned with the vision and mission.

When Your Senior Leaders Are Supportive But Don't Know How to Get Started

Dr. Katherine Gottlieb, CEO of Southcentral Foundation (a Baldrige Award health care recipient in 2011), described exploring the Baldrige Criteria with her VPs and the board in 2003. "We knew it would cost us time, cost us money. But we came to an agreement that this [using the Baldrige framework] would be the tool to drive systematic change." She also found that developing the Organizational Profile—the five-page description of what an organization does, how it functions, and its competitive environment—was a driving force for gaining leadership buy-in from the VPs and the managers as they provided input and feedback to document who Southcentral Foundation was.

Several leaders talked about the value of taking board members and other senior leaders to the Baldrige Quest for Excellence® Conference as a way to increase their understanding and to get them excited about the journey by hearing the lessons learned and best practices of Baldrige Award recipients.

Some leaders describe as part of the problem with getting started the Baldrige Criteria themselves. While written in English, many people reading them for the first time are overwhelmed by their complexity and unique use of some common terminology. Some organizations send people to become examiners to build in-house capability and familiarity with the framework and terminology. (See Chapter 14, "Lessons Learned About the Journey," on the value of being an examiner and having others in the organization become examiners.) Some start with tiered levels and assistance provided by their state or regional Baldrige-based programs. (See Chapter 14 for more on the value of the state and regional programs.) Others hire experienced Baldrige consultants.

Several of the senior leaders emphasized the need to bring in Baldrige expertise early in the journey. David Ramsey, CEO of Charleston Area Medical Center (a 2015 Baldrige Award recipient), said, "An organization can't learn the Criteria overnight. We didn't understand the integration across the categories. You've got to bring on an advisor. Someone who can 'translate' the Criteria."

Administrators from Maine Veterans' Homes (Scarborough, Caribou, and Machias, respectively) on the AHCA/NCAL Quality Award journey emphasized the need for help in understanding the Criteria. (MVH-Scarborough was named a Gold Award recipient in August 2016.) Maureen Carland said, "Work with somebody who truly knows the Criteria. It's a new language, and you cannot expect to know it all at first." Melissa Graham shared, "Without a coach, we spent hours answering one question because we really didn't understand it." Marcia Jackson concluded, "We applied for our Silver Award without a coach. We wouldn't have even attempted Gold without a coach. A coach helps you understand, 'What is this question asking, and how do I need to respond to it in a way that answers the Criteria and meets the Scoring Guidelines?'"

What we *don't* recommend is that organizations without any knowledge of the Baldrige Criteria, the application process, and the assessment process jump in, flail around in the deep end of the pool, and expect to get much out of the effort. Even those organizations that aren't expecting to receive the award are not likely to get much value from the feedback. If the application isn't well written and reflective of the organization, the examiners are limited in what insight they might otherwise provide.

Getting Nonemployed Physicians on Board in a Health Care System

In her book *On Becoming Exceptional*, Sister Mary Jean Ryan (former CEO of SSM Health Care, the first health care recipient of the Baldrige Award in 2002) says, "Most physicians work in remarkable isolation. They often have no idea how their hospital performs as a whole—even in their own practice area. So when they are shown data documenting that the hospital's performance is not what it should be, they are both startled and displeased."[2]

In Chapter 5, we discussed how leaders of Baldrige Award-winning organizations have used data to drive engagement. Dr. Rulon Stacey, former CEO of Poudre Valley Health System (a Baldrige Award recipient in 2008), admits that getting the organization's nonemployed physicians on board was an area where it could have done a better job, and some of that included more extensive sharing of the system's data.

In the organization's 10-year journey to becoming award-worthy, he says, "In the first few years, we informed them [the nonemployed physicians], but we didn't engage them. That really delayed our progress." The feedback from the first site visit from the state's Baldrige-based program essentially said, "You really haven't engaged your physicians." Rulon continued, "Although we had done better than anyone else in the country at creating good economic partnerships with our physicians, we hadn't engaged them in the Baldrige process. When the feedback referred to them as part of our workforce, well, that was really the first time we began to think of them as a key component of our workforce although they weren't employed by us. We hired a chief medical officer, Dr. William Neff. In our initial strategy process the second year, we had about 80 directors, managers, and others in the meeting. Dr. Neff asked, 'How many of these folks are physicians?' Oops! Point taken." The elected medical staff leaders became involved in the most intimate board discussions and strategies. Transparency became the rule. "Nothing was off limits for them." A white paper published by the Physician Leadership Institute, *Integrated Leaders Build a Culture of Trust*, states,

"Without trust, there is no alignment, without alignment, there is no engagement, and without engagement, there can be no transformation. Functional trust-based partnerships between physicians and hospital executives hinge upon the ability of each partner to work together, in service of shared clinical and business priorities."[3]

During the press conference announcing Poudre Valley Health System's Baldrige Award, Dr. Neff described the difference these partnerships made. "Other systems treat physicians as competitors. We have learned to trust and collaborate with each other, and this has allowed us to grow quicker and be more successful."

As the organization continued its journey and began to employ physicians, it got more insightful feedback. "If you were an employed physician, you went through the system's new employee orientation, which included a lot on our vision, mission, and values. If you were an independent physician, you went through an entirely different orientation. Yet we expected both types of physicians to take care of patients the same way—the Poudre Valley way. Getting that feedback really opened our eyes." The organization began ensuring that both types of new physicians received the same focus on the vision, mission, and values.

Brian Dieter, president and CEO of Mary Greeley Medical Center (a 2014 recipient of the Gold Award from the Iowa Recognition for Performance Excellence), said getting the independent physicians was important but involved not trumpeting out a program. Brian explained, "Eventually you get to where the doctors see that things are going on that make their delivery of care easier. You get their buy-in when you demonstrate results." Karen Kiel Rosser, vice president and quality officer for the same organization, added, "They see our medical center's data. We are much more intentional about sharing our dashboard with them on a quarterly basis.

We make it clear how they impact those measures and help us achieve important improvements."

When You Face Skepticism

Harry Zechman, COO, and Rob Ecklin, president of Stoner, Inc. (a Baldrige Award small business recipient in 2003), said they didn't encounter outright resistance but saw skepticism. "Part of it was that it seemed so far-fetched that we could compete at the national level. [At the time they had 43 full- and 5 part-time employees.] The other part was it seemed like extra work."

After attending a Baldrige Quest for Excellence® Conference, they learned from some of the leaders from Baldrige Award recipients about how they managed the journey. When they returned home, they assigned their senior leaders as Category Champions. This accomplished several things. First, it ensured that the senior leaders became personally familiar with the Baldrige Criteria. Second, the senior leaders began to incorporate what they were learning as part of their approach to managing the business, so that it wasn't additional work. Finally, the time and commitment of the senior leaders was a visible symbol to the rest of the organization about the seriousness of this journey.

Rob said, "It took a while, but we explained to the group that Baldrige was going to be the way we ran the business." Harry agreed and added, "There's a feeling that ultimately becomes a very positive one when people see the business system improvements or the gaps that you're addressing are somehow related to Baldrige, or they see an improvement in a process that makes their job or life easier." As time went on, the skepticism turned to enthusiasm and pride.

Diane Brockmeier, CEO of Mid-America Transplant Services (a 2015 Baldrige Award recipient), says that the skepticism actually started to form about four or five years into the journey. She and the senior leaders said, "We don't have time to do two sets of work. We were operating in parallel tracks—one was how we ran the business and the second was 'doing Baldrige.' We had to figure out how to do our work using the Baldrige framework, and we did. Everything became process-driven. We started with our Clinical Department and expanded the approach to all of the other areas. We became much more systematic, and we held our people accountable to being systematic. When that happened, we found that we could reproduce high-quality results over time."

Brian Dieter acknowledged that he faced what he terms "healthy" skepticism. He added, "You have to create a safe environment for leaders to express that. One thing that helped was our messaging. We didn't have a big rollout with posters and other stuff. We just described beginning our journey to our senior leaders as a way of involving our staff in decision making and focusing on our processes." Karen Kiel Rosser said, "We were on the journey for several years before our employees even knew we were on the journey. We had focused on continuous process improvement and what it meant to the employees—helping them make their own work better every day and why the work we do is important."

When You Face Open Resistance

Tommy Gonzalez, former city manager of the City of Irving (a Baldrige Award government recipient in 2012), described some early resistance. "People who have been in an organization for 20-plus years become cynical. Even more so in a government organization." He focused on constantly communicating the reason for using the Baldrige framework—to drive improvement—and using data as a way to compel the senior leaders to see why this approach made sense. He also found that "a lot of folks on this kind of journey miss the middle layer. That's the group that will kill you if you don't get them on board. These are the people who directly lead the people who are the backbone of the organization." Most of middle managers' concerns center around a fear of losing their own power if they empower their employees. Tommy addressed these concerns with direct communication, engaging with the middle managers in frank, two-way conversations. He also made sure that when he looked at making improvements in the organization, he included resolving issues that were important to the managers. "You connect with employees at an intellectual and emotional level and by delivering results. Middle managers are no different. They know if you are listening to them."

Dr. Mike Sather, former director of Veterans Affairs Cooperative Studies Program Clinical Research Coordinating Center (VACSP) (a Baldrige Award government recipient in 2009), laughed when asked if any of his senior leaders resisted going on the Baldrige journey. "All of them. They were very busy with a heavy workload. Several of the leaders confronted me with, 'Do you want me to do my job or this Baldrige stuff?'" He replied that he wanted them to do both but also to change the way they did their jobs.

Dr. David Spong is the retired leader of two different Boeing divisions to receive the Baldrige Award (Boeing Mobility—formerly Airlift & Tanker [A&T] in the manufacturing category in 1998 and Boeing Support Systems—formerly Aerospace Support in the service category in 2003). He is also, to date, the only person to lead organizations in two different categories to win the Baldrige Award.

David personally understood the resistance some of his senior leaders at Aerospace Support expressed. He had felt the same cynicism when he was with McDonnell Douglas and the use of Baldrige was mandated by John McDonnell. He admits, "I thought it was a lot of phooey, but as a senior leader, I realized I had to act like I believed it. Acting like I believed, led to doing. Once you do that and see the improvement happening, it becomes easy to believe." He challenged his handful of resisters to likewise at least act as if they believed, and ultimately they, too, became proponents.

Dale Crownover, CEO of Texas Nameplate Company, Inc. (a Baldrige Award small business recipient in 1998 and 2004), became convinced that he wanted to use Baldrige, but he really wasn't sure why. The company was struggling, and he knew he had to do something different. At the time, Six Sigma and ISO really didn't have any traction with small companies. Some of his senior leaders resisted using Baldrige. Dale's approach was, "I won't terminate you, and I hope you'll go along with it. If you don't want to do it, just don't get in the way."

It turned out there were other people in the organization who wanted to take the company in the same direction. As Dale said, "They saw it as an opportunity to grow with the company. Even now, people see success and want to be part of that success."

Dr. Bruce Kintz, CEO of Concordia Publishing House (a Baldrige Award nonprofit recipient in 2011), encountered some initial resistance, but he practiced patience to get everyone on board. His approach was to be personally engaged in briefing the whole company, 25 people at a time. He also spent time garnering trust by listening when someone told him about a barrier to being able to improve a process, and he began "knocking down those walls."

When You Face Passive-Aggressive Resistance

Terry May, founder and CEO of MESA Products, Inc. (Baldrige Award small business recipient in 2006 and 2012), says that it took the entire five years in their first venture to get all of the

senior leaders on board. Initially, there was a lot of "head nod-
ding because none of us really understood what was involved
and how it would affect us," but the passive resistance began
in the second and third year. As a senior leader, he needed to
decide whether to ride it out or pull the trigger (ask people to
leave the organization). "As we got engaged in the journey, I
had a couple of leaders who weren't sure they wanted to make
the changes required." Ultimately, they all were on board for
the journey.

For their second attempt for a repeat award, Terry needed
to engage new senior leaders who had joined the organization
since their first journey and award. However, he described
this time as being much easier because when the new senior
leaders joined the organization, "They looked around, and
they viewed what they saw as 'normal.' When you bring someone through the journey, that's a huge change. The people
who joined us after 2006 just see it [Baldrige] as the way we
do business."

Like Tommy Gonzalez, Terry also acknowledged the need
to get middle managers and supervisors on board. Senior
leaders' attention to these groups was key to the organization's successful use of the Baldrige framework as the way to
run the business.

David Tilton of AtlantiCare explained that when you
have a senior leadership team that is engaged personally in
using the Baldrige framework to improve the organization, it
becomes pretty obvious when one or two senior leaders aren't
doing the work. "A CEO's job is to weed the garden. Of the
22 people on the senior leadership team, only 2 were asked
to leave. However, when I asked people to leave, it made the
rest of the organization aware of how committed I was to this
journey."

Ken Schnitzer, chairman of Park Place Dealerships
(the parent organization of Park Place Lexus, the only car

dealership to win the Baldrige Award, 2005), said that all of his senior leaders resisted a bit when he said they were going on this journey. "However, getting them to really *buy in* was a whole other issue. I was really getting lip service. They would do just enough to stay out of trouble, but nothing more. I finally had to sit down with a few people and be blunt. They either needed to get on the bus or get off the bus. And that meant as a senior leader in the organization, they had to personally lead and also hold their managers accountable." Ken also admits that part of the problem was that in his first five or six years with the organization, he tried a lot of different things but didn't stick with anything. The senior leaders and the rest of the organization thought that this interest in Baldrige would also go away. He had to demonstrate his own commitment to this journey to convince the skeptics.

Using Crisis to Your Advantage

Joe Brescia, director of strategic management and process improvement of the U.S. Army Armament Research, Development and Engineering Center (ARDEC) (a Baldrige Award government recipient in 2007), described how ARDEC's senior leaders got on board. "Well, nothing focuses your attention and effort like narrowly averting a crisis." Back in 1995, ARDEC had just survived a very "close call" with DoD's base realignment and closure (BRAC). In response, ARDEC's commanding general, General James Boddie, provided the necessary vision and influence to convince the senior leadership team and the workforce why change was needed, what it would look like, and how it would be achieved. He then assigned ARDEC's top executives to serve as Baldrige Category Champions to drive improvements. He also provided the necessary training for participants and established ARDEC's Quality Management Executive Council to institutionalize, guide, and monitor ARDEC's continuous improvement efforts across the organization.

David Spong describes a similar situation in the first Boeing division he led to receive a Baldrige Award. "In 1991, the C-17 program was in deep trouble. We had not yet delivered any aircraft and were at least six months behind our production schedule. We had poor quality and were about $1.2 billion overrun of our own money on a fixed-price development contract, with the U.S. Government contract overrun by a similar amount."[4]

David goes on to explain, "When your organization is in a crisis, you will try any approach that might help your organization improve. We were doing many good things in the organization, but what we needed was a framework to help us focus our resources and to integrate the improvements." Baldrige was that framework.[5]

When You Encounter Early Disappointment

Dr. Joe Alexander, former dean of the Kenneth W. Monfort College of Business (a Baldrige Award education recipient in 2004), described that the senior leaders who had adopted pursuing the Baldrige journey as the school's BHAG (Big Hairy Audacious Goal) in 2002 were initially very excited since no other business school had achieved the award. However, a few of them felt insulted when the organization's first application scored around 300 points (out of 1,000).

However, as they continued to pursue their Baldrige journey, Dr. Alexander found that customers, students, and other stakeholders were "impressed that we were choosing a standard of excellence far above any other standard with which they would hold you accountable. They were coming in and asking how they could help. There's something contagious about wanting to be the best at something."

As we have worked with dozens and dozens of clients on their performance excellence journeys, we've watched many senior leaders struggle with getting consensus from the other senior leaders to commit to the journey. However, our experience has been that while initial reluctance can be tolerated, ongoing resistance—either active or passive—cannot be permitted over time. That resistance creates dysfunctionality not only among the senior leadership team but throughout the organization as well. Once the course has been set, everyone needs to pull in the same direction.

Getting All of the Senior Leaders on Board—Checklist

1. How will you frame your decision to embark on a journey to performance excellence?
2. How can you provide support to your team in understanding the Criteria?
3. If you're in health care, what approaches will you take to get nonemployed physicians on board?
4. How will you deal with open resistance, passive resistance, and/or skepticism?
5. How could you use crisis to your advantage?

Confronting a Culture
of Entitlement

- Attending to bad relationships
- Using data to confront entitlement
- Using incentives to change a culture of entitlement
- Don't accept continued poor performance

Entitlement is an unwarranted expectation of favorable conditions and preferential treatment. In some cases, it has developed over time due to unchecked demands from employees. In other cases, it stems from protective contractual relationships such as are seen in the public sector with strong civil service rules and in some unionized workforces. In either case, a culture of entitlement is incompatible with an intent to lead an organization in the pursuit of excellence.

In recent years, we've seen a change in some grade schools that don't keep score in games because they want to protect every student's self-esteem by letting everybody be a "winner." Whether you support that philosophy or not for raising children, it's simply not a credible approach in business. Organizations, whether for-profit or not-for-profit, must deliver results to survive. And they must keep score against their competition. However, in organizations with a culture of entitlement, employees aren't held accountable for the results of the business and feel no responsibility for the organization's success. In fact, in some cases, the demands of an entitled workforce have actually led to the failure of an organization as was seen in 2012 with the bankruptcy filing by Hostess and the more recent filing by A&P in 2015 when both companies were unable to reach agreements on union demands.

We've also seen a shift in employees' mindsets with the return of a more favorable economic environment. In the downturn in 2008 through 2010, the prevailing attitude of employees was gratitude in having and keeping a job. Today, the mindset seems to have shifted for many workers to "my organization should be grateful it has me!"

If a new senior leader has been brought in to execute a turnaround and the organization has an entrenched culture of entitlement, change and confrontation is inevitable. The same is true when a new senior leader comes into an organization where he or she wants to create a culture of performance excellence. This is the time for the new leader to reset expectations, but it may also call for educating employees on the fundamentals of business. In an interview with Brad Hams, founder and president of Ownership Thinking, Jim McElgunn, senior editor of *PROFIT* magazine, asked why it was crucial to teach employees how the company makes money. Hams's response was eye-opening. "In some recent employee training, I asked a group of them, 'What percentage of the company's $120 million in revenue do you think was profit?' It's very common for employees to guess 35 to 50%. But we've never worked with a client that made 50% profit, and this client's profit was actually 0.2%!"[1] Imagine how the mistaken assumption by the employees led to wastefulness and demands for higher wages and more benefits.

Hams goes on in the interview to explain how important the use of making measurement of day-to-day activities visible to the workforce is, which is related to the transparency described in Chapter 5. "This forces employees to learn about the impact their part of the company has on the whole, and shows them the correlation between what they do and the financial impact on the company."[2] This approach was used successfully to engage the workforce by leaders of Baldrige Award recipient organizations and is described in Chapter 5 and in another example later in this chapter.

One of the ways that Zappos counters entitlement is with an explicit focus on its core values that begins during the recruitment and hiring process and continues during new hire training. "After the four-week training period, everyone is offered one month's pay to quit. The pay-to-quit offer makes new employees really think about if they feel Zappos is the right place for them, and if they are right for Zappos. Less than 1% take the offer annually."[3] This emphasis on the organization's values is something we saw leaders of Baldrige Award recipients do in Chapter 3.

The importance of forging alliances with labor unions is underscored by research conducted by Gallup and reported in September 2009. The research included meta-analysis of responses from 125 organizations—both unionized and non-unionized—on the 12 statements (the Gallup Q^{12} that have proven correlation with employee engagement). Jessica Tyler reports in an article for the *Gallup Business Journal*, "In the U.S. working population, 20% of those who report being in a union are engaged, while 27% of those who report not being in a union are engaged."[4] Even in the more than 500 organizations with which Gallup consults on employee engagement, the discrepancy persists. Tyler continues, "38% of union employees are engaged. 45% of non-union employees are engaged. . . . 34% of union workgroups, compared to 26% of non-union workgroups, are in the bottom quartile of Gallup's global employee engagement database. Groups in the bottom quartile are considered low performing—not only for engagement, but for business outcomes as well." These levels of engagement and the repercussions for productivity were described in Chapter 2.

Our next leader of a Baldrige Award–winning organization understood the importance of getting the union workforce engaged in a critical turnaround situation.

Attending to Bad Relationships

Dr. David Spong is the retired leader of two different Boeing divisions to receive the Baldrige Award (Boeing Mobility—formerly Airlift & Tanker [A&T] in the manufacturing category in 1998 and Boeing Support Systems—formerly Aerospace Support in the service category in 2003).

Prior to David's taking over the helm at Boeing A&T, there had been a history of a very bad relationship with the union. It was easy to become defensive with union members in an environment of constant complaints and grievances. David's boss began working to change this relationship, and David continued this effort as he moved into the senior leadership ranks. One approach was having a genuine open door policy. Since David arrived at work earlier than his boss (then the head of Boeing A&T) and had his door open, employees would come to him with their gripes. According to him, "I was the only one there on 'mahogany row,' so I was the one to attack. Usually I had no idea what they were talking about with their complaint, but I'd ask who they worked for and on up their chain of command until I knew the person. And then I'd go investigate with that person. In the early days, I often found that something indeed was wrong, that we had not treated someone properly. And we would fix it." Over time, the union began to see that management was not only willing to listen but to act. David continued, "And this led to more improvement as we received more feedback and ideas from them."

Using Data to Confront Entitlement

David continued to explain that the use of data was also key to engaging the employees. When all manufacturing and assembly cells on the factory floor had their charts showing their on-time delivery, quality results, and schedule performance, they took ownership for the processes. "The culture was palpable with the enthusiasm of the people and the teams. People would show the data that they were using and talk with pride about what they had achieved," explained David.

Using Incentives to Change a Culture of Entitlement

Boeing A&T also implemented a program working with the union called Employee Involvement (subsequently renamed to Employee Engagement). Later, they added gainsharing that rewarded a group with a bonus for beating its budget. These became instrumental in the team-based culture that was created and noted in the profile of the organization when it won the Baldrige Award.

In an article in *Harvard Business Review* published in 2014, Robert Lavigna describes eight factors that make motivating government employees difficult. These are:

- "Prevailing negative attitudes about government and government employees
- Frequent and abrupt changes in leadership
- Hard-to-measure achievement
- An older workforce
- Strong civil-service rules and employee protections

- Constraints on the use of financial incentives
- Strong union influence
- Public visibility of government"[5]

Tommy Gonzalez, former city manager of the City of Irving (a Baldrige Award government recipient in 2012), described the culture of entitlement he faced when he took on the job. The eight factors listed above were all at play. As he explains, "People felt like they had a job until they retired. In the private sector—unlike the public sector—there are often perks and incentives." By developing the Playbook, described in Chapter 3, he was able to connect every employee with the goals of the organization and how progress was measured with the key performance indicators (KPIs).

Tommy decided that if his team members implemented Lean Six Sigma (LSS) and generated sufficient savings he could convince the City Council to approve incentive programs and pay raises, even during the recession and even in a government organization. And that's exactly what they did. Employees got incentives for participating in the wellness programs where their healthier lifestyles saved the city money. Once LSS teams completed a project and savings were validated, each team member received $100. Over eight years, the organization saved more than $77 million, which easily offset the cost of incentives and pay raises.

The results of a highly engaged workforce also showed up in the measures of satisfaction by the city's residents. From the time the city began its journey to performance excellence until it received the award in 2012, the percentage of residents rating key services—including police, code enforcement, libraries, and recreation—as good or excellent increased by double digits. Jessica Tyler from the Gallup observes, "Engaged public servants can move the needle of public opinion about government, one interaction at a time."[6]

Michael Levinson, former city manager, City of Coral Springs (in 2007, the first Baldrige Award recipient in government), offers his testimonial. "People ask, 'Why Baldrige?' My answer is very simple: a Triple A bond rating on Wall Street from all three rating agencies, bringing capital projects in on time and within budget, a 96 percent business satisfaction rating, a 94 percent resident satisfaction rating, an overall quality rating of 95 percent, and an employee satisfaction rating of 97 percent . . . that's why we're involved with Baldrige.

"A corporate management model is absolutely necessary in government. We in government live in a slew of production functions. The challenge is to harness all those resources, point them in the direction of your customers, and provide the goods and services to your community in the most responsive and responsible way.

"We . . . see a number of cities around the country that are beginning to focus on the Baldrige Criteria and take a holistic approach to performance excellence. . . . We are forming a consortium for benchmarking purposes and comparing data. . . . More and more cities and local governments are joining on to look at best practices and to compare their results with other high performing cities. It's great for government in America."

Don't Accept Continued Poor Performance

One of the other aspects of confronting a culture of entitlement is addressing poor performers. Engaged employees are high performers, and they want their peers to be held accountable. They want to work with team members they can count on and who can help the whole organization's performance improve. It is demotivating for good performers to watch obvious poor performance go unaddressed and without consequences.

Ken Schiller, cofounder and co-owner of K&N Management (a Baldrige Award small business recipient in 2010), stated, "As senior leaders, you must reward the behavior you want. Top performers at all levels of the organization are recognized for innovation and results. Team members who are not meeting standards, regardless of tenure, are put on improvement plans. If they continue to underperform, they are redeployed or transferred to a different position . . . or to a different organization."

Confronting a Culture of Entitlement—Checklist

1. Does your organization have a culture of entitlement? If yes, what are the signs?
2. Does your organization have employees represented by a bargaining unit? If yes, what is the relationship like between the union(s) and management? How could it be improved?
3. How can you share more data to help people see the value of their work?
4. What incentives could you create that would allow employees to reap some of the benefits for improving customer satisfaction and increasing productivity?

Employee Engagement and the Bottom Line

Study after study that we read cites clear correlation between increasing employee engagement and improving performance in results that matter to successful organizations. Some of these findings were provided in Chapter 2. The senior leaders we interviewed for this book all expressed their conviction that having an engaged workforce led to exceptional results and a competitive advantage. Some of those exceptional results are presented later in this chapter.

Engagement and Patient and Employee Safety

Within the health care industry, more and more emphasis is being placed on ensuring patient safety. What is important to note is that research has shown that patient safety and employee engagement are correlated. One measure of employee engagement is turnover—or the lack thereof. "According to the Voluntary Hospital Association, if employee turnover is below 12 percent, the organization's mortality index is much lower and length of stay is shorter than those with over 12 percent turnover. Low staff turnover saves lives."[1]

What has also been found to be true is that a focus on employee engagement leads to a safer workplace, and that results in improved patient safety. A study published in the *Journal of Patient Safety*, "Workplace Engagement and Workers' Compensation Claims as Predictors for Patient Safety Culture,"[2] found that "a synergistic effect exists between employee engagement and decreased levels of workers' compensation claims for improving patient safety culture."

Additional research by Gallup and Loma Linda University Medical Center "shows that employee engagement and employee safety work together to enhance patient safety. When healthcare employees work in a safe environment and are engaged, the chances are much greater that they will perform activities that are now drivers of patient safety outcomes better."[3] In Gallup's State of the Global Workplace report, researchers found that work units in the top quartile in employee engagement had 48 percent fewer safety incidents and 41 percent fewer patient safety incidents.[4]

Paul Worstell, former CEO of PRO-TEC Coating Company (a 2007 Baldrige Award small business recipient), describes the value of the Baldrige journey in increasing employee engagement and achieving unprecedented safety performance in a very challenging manufacturing environment that included a 24/7 work schedule. "We knew we had an engaged workforce with less than 1% turnover rate and absenteeism at 0.6%. Safety was always a first priority. We used our Baldrige activity to earn the rigorous OSHA VP Star the first time we applied for it."

On December 29, 2014, the company marked 10 years since its last lost work day (more than 5.4 million man-hours), and the record continues. It finished the same year with zero OSHA recordable incidents, and that record continues. The company even extends its zeal for a safe workplace to its contractors working on-site who have also gone for the last two years without an OSHA recordable incident. This amazing safety performance was achieved at the same time the organization opened a new facility that resulted in a 33 percent increase in its workforce and a 50 percent increase in product capacity.[5] (See Appendix A for a link to a video of their safety culture.)

Engagement and Job Growth

Fortune has been awarding the 100 Best Companies to Work For status for 19 years. In that time, 13 companies have appeared on every list. In the first 18 years, those companies created 341,567 new jobs, or job growth of 172 percent.[6] Similar impact has been demonstrated by researching those seven organizations that have won the Baldrige Award twice. They boast a 63 percent median job growth compared with 3.5 percent for a matched set of industries and time periods.

Engagement and Profitability

In a study of 76 midscale hotels of the same brand, approximately 6,800 employees were surveyed. Trust in leadership's integrity was determined to have the strongest correlation ($r = 0.36$) with employee engagement. What was even more striking was the finding that moving engagement up by only one-quarter of a point on a 10-point scale led to an additional $250,000 of profit for one hotel, or 2.5 percent of the revenue.[7] This correlation has also been demonstrated by the seven organizations that have won the Baldrige Award twice that achieved a 92 percent median growth in revenue.

Further Evidence from Some of the Baldrige Award Recipients

ARDEC

At the time it received the award in 2007, ARDEC's levels for workforce engagement (empowerment, communication, motivation, training, and recognition) were consistently ranked above 80 percent by employees and were higher than comparable best-in-class benchmarks. Job satisfaction increased from 85 percent in fiscal year 2004 to 90 percent in fiscal year 2007, exceeding American Productivity and Quality Center (APQC) and best-in-class benchmarks.

The results from this engaged workforce? ARDEC had achieved overall Lean/Six Sigma improvements in quality (91 percent), cost (70 percent), schedule (67 percent), and risk (84 percent) with an overall cost avoidance of $3.22 billion since 2001. The organization was also recognized for the technological innovation of its SWORDS robot that was named one of the "most amazing inventions of 2004" by *Time* magazine.

Charleston Area Medical Center (CAMC)

CAMC demonstrates its workforce engagement with a turnover rate better than the U.S. benchmark set by Nursing Solutions, Inc., a national hospital staffing service, since 2010. Results from this engaged workforce include achieving top decile for patient safety in 2013 and 2104, top decile nationally for outpatient satisfaction in all areas, and top decile nationally for its patient satisfaction with the discharge process. CAMC's Sepsis Performance Improvement Team saved 1,798 lives from 2011 to 2014, better than the Premier national top decile level since 2012.

In addition, involving engaged employees in process improvement has resulted in taking $177 million out of CAMC's budget over the past 15 years, with last year accounting for $21 million of those total savings.

Concordia Publishing House

When this organization received the award in 2011, workforce satisfaction with senior leaders had been above the AAIM (formerly known as the American Association of Industrial Management for Employers Association) national benchmark since 2007. Overall workforce engagement had exceeded the AAIM benchmark in seven out of eight categories for the past three cycles.

This highly engaged workforce produced overall customer satisfaction scores at 98 percent plus, exceeding levels set forth by the annual *Purdue University Benchmark Study of U.S. Call Centers.*

Mid-America Transplant Services (MTS)

With an overall workplace engagement of about 80 percent, MTS has met or exceeded national best-in-class comparisons since 2012. One hundred percent of its employees strongly agree that they have a connection to the organization's mission since 2011, setting the national benchmark. Employee retention rate approaches 90 percent and has exceeded the Association of Organ Procurement Organizations' average since 2012.

This very engaged workforce not only demonstrates better performance than the industry best-in-class reported benchmark of 2 percent missed organ referrals with a 0.08 percent rate since 2012, it also generates gross revenue and net margin better than industry benchmarks since 2012.

MidwayUSA

In Chapter 14, we talk about CEO of MidwayUSA, Larry Potterfield, and his indisputable commitment to the Baldrige journey as evidenced by his investment in developing leaders in the organizations by having them train and serve as examiners at state and national programs. These staggering numbers are shown in Figure 12.1.

When this organization received its first Baldrige award in 2009, results for indicators of workforce engagement and satisfaction in its contact center, as well as employee satisfaction in its merchandising, marketing, and logistics departments, showed levels comparable with national benchmark performance ratings of 77 percent and 80 percent, respectively. The organization maintained its focus on employee engagement with its last survey showing 83 percent. Figure 12.2 shows that this high level of engagement has been sustained.

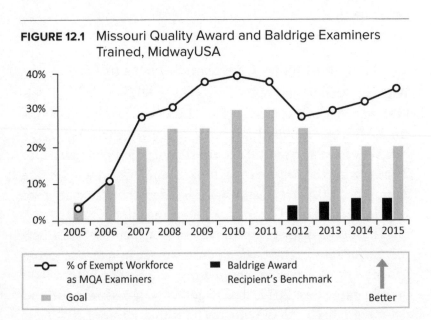

FIGURE 12.1 Missouri Quality Award and Baldrige Examiners Trained, MidwayUSA

FIGURE 12.2   Employee Satisfaction and Engagement, MidwayUSA

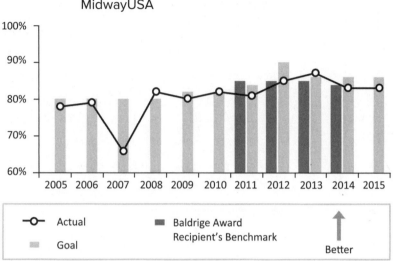

Satisfied and engaged employees delight customers. Customer approval ratings have topped 90 percent since 2006 and have been better than the performance of its primary Internet retailing competitor for the past two years. In addition, customer retention is 23 percent better than the national benchmark for Internet retailers.

Delighted customers help the organization achieve strong financial performance. Since 2004, the company has sustained a 43.8 percent average annual growth rate in net income and a 21.3 percent average annual growth rate in gross sales, making it one of the fastest-growing companies in its industry. This impressive financial performance was sustained even during the economic downturn of 2008–2009.

And similar to what Paul Worstell described about the relationship between employee engagement and workforce safety, Larry Potterfield demonstrates that an increased emphasis on safety coupled with an engaged workforce leads to world-class performance, shown in Figure 12.3.

FIGURE 12.3 Number of Days Away from Work and Restricted Days, MidwayUSA

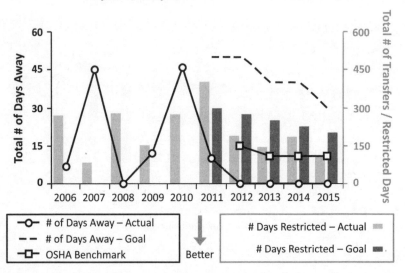

Elevations Credit Union (ECU)

Receiving the Baldrige award in 2014, this organization is dedicated to being "the best place you have ever worked." Since 2011, ECU has recorded positive trends in engagement and satisfaction, with employees feeling ECU "has a winning team" increasing from 68 percent in 2011 to 85 percent in 2014; "builds careers" increasing from 58 percent to 70 percent; "makes me proud to be part of this organization" increasing from 82 percent to 90 percent; and "gives me the responsibility and freedom to do my job" increasing from 77 percent to 88 percent.

The positive trend in overall engagement shown in Figure 12.4 demonstrates that ECU is in the "Very Good/Great" level that few organizations can achieve.

Gerry Agnes, president and CEO of ECU, says, "Our financial results are the by-product of employees serving our

FIGURE 12.4   Percent of Workforce Engaged, Elevations Credit Union

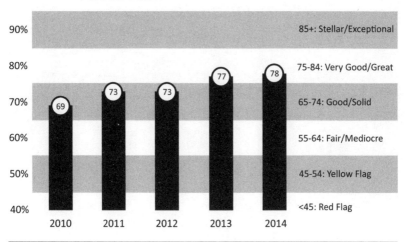

members and doing a great job. My job as CEO is to turn this organization over to the next CEO in better shape than it is today, and through the Baldrige framework, we'll be able to do that."

Through its systematic process management and improvement and its engaged workforce, ECU has been named "Best Financial Institution" by readers of the *Boulder Daily Camera* for 15 of the past 16 years, and repeatedly as "Best Bank," "Best Mortgage Company," or "Best Customer Service" by readers of the *Colorado Daily, Boulder Weekly, Longmont Times-Call*, and *Loveland Reporter-Herald*.

MESA Products, Inc.

When this small business won its second Baldrige Award in 2012, employee satisfaction and engagement were significantly better than that of its best competitor. Since that time, the company continues to outperform its best competitor

FIGURE 12.5 Employee Overall Satisfaction and Engagement (Enthusiasm), MESA Products

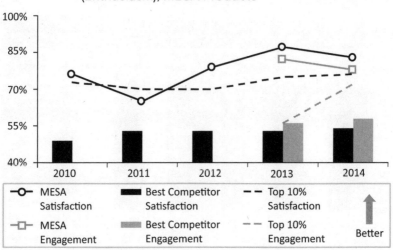

and is better than top decile performance, as shown in Figure 12.5.

Customer retention rates consistently exceeded 95 percent in both materials and service between 2006 and 2011, and revenue from existing customers increased over the same period. The customer satisfaction index has been at high levels since 2006, increasing from 87 percent in 2006 to over 90 percent since 2009; these levels are consistently better than competitors (ranging from 72 to 83 percent) and the American Customer Satisfaction Index (ranging from 72 to 76 percent).

According to a third-party survey, MESA leads its competitors in customer satisfaction. In 2012, MESA led its closest competitor in 20 out of 20 performance attributes, resulting in an industry benchmark placement in the top 1 percent.

FIGURE 12.6   Involvement and Engagement,
Pewaukee School District

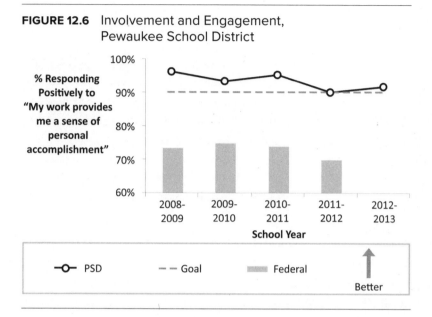

Pewaukee School District (PSD)

PSD was named by the *Milwaukee Journal Sentinel* as one of Wisconsin's Top 100 Workplaces for the years 2011 through 2013. Staff satisfaction was 73.1 percent for salaries, 81.5 percent with benefits, and 91.6 percent with engagement and involvement—all far exceeding the national averages. Positive responses to "My work provides me a sense of personal accomplishment" are significantly higher than the comparison, as shown in Figure 12.6.

A satisfied and engaged workforce helps students achieve academically. Despite having one of the most rigorous public school graduation requirements (28 credits) in the state, PSD achieved a 97.4 percent graduation rate in 2012–2013 and had a higher graduation rate from 2008 through 2012 than other county, state, and nearby high-performing districts. PSD's low dropout rate of 0.09 percent is better than those of the county, state, and nearby high-performing districts by a factor of 5 to 15.

Surveys also showed PSD parent satisfaction with communication ranged between 91.5 percent and 94.8 percent at the four schools in 2012–2013, while the national average was 74 percent. Parent satisfaction with educational quality during the same school year was 93.8 percent.

The City of Irving

Irving's 2012 employee survey results show that its employee ratings exceeded the highest comparable score received by a U.S. government agency. For example, 95 percent of Irving employees said the city government was a good place to work compared to a federal agency high of 84 percent. In addition, city employees who participate in Irving's incentive-driven "I Win" wellness program can earn monthly pay incentives ranging from $50 to $150 per month for one year based on their annual physical fitness and medical test scores. The program, which has been recognized by the American Heart Association, has helped the city address rising health care costs and helped employees reduce health care risks. The city has saved an estimated $1.5 million in medical claim costs annually and reduced its actuarial-determined retiree health insurance cost by $25 million over a 25-year period.

In addition, a highly engaged workforce is reflected by a decreasing turnover rate that is significantly better than the city's best local competitor, shown in Figure 12.7.

What does this engaged workforce do for the city's residents? Provide extraordinary service while operating efficiently. The rating for overall quality of service in Irving (74 percent) is higher than the state of Texas (46 percent),

FIGURE 12.7 Comparative Employee Turnover Rate, City of Irving

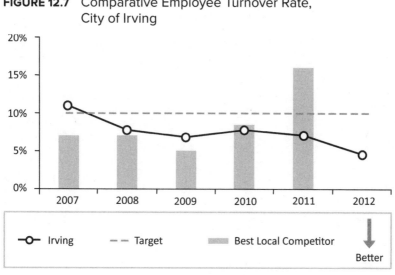

county government (37 percent), and the U.S. government (38 percent). Since 2006, the percentage of residents rating many of the city's key services—including police, code enforcement, libraries, and recreational—as good or excellent has increased by double digits. Surveys have shown that the percentage of citizens who feel that overall quality of life has improved has increased from 52 percent in 2006 to 71 percent in 2012.

Fiscal achievement is at a benchmark level, too. The City of Irving is one of 5 cities in the state and 89 in the nation with a AAA rating from both Standard and Poor's (S&P) and Moody's—ratings that it has maintained since 2007. Irving's tax rate is the second lowest in the Dallas–Fort Worth metropolitan area. Since 2007, its overall cost of service—combining property tax, water, sewer, drainage, and sanitation charges—has been better than four comparable cities in the area.

FIGURE 12.8　Staff Voluntary Turnover Rate, Poudre Valley Health System

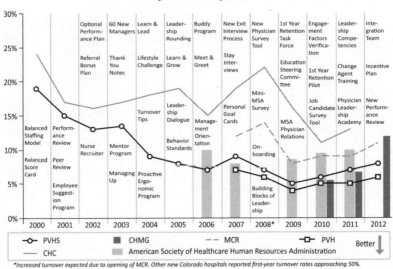

Increased turnover expected due to opening of MCR. Other new Colorado hospitals reported first-year turnover rates approaching 50%.

Poudre Valley Health System (PVH) (Now University of Colorado Health System)

For five consecutive years, PVH was one of seven U.S. hospitals to be named a Thomson 100 Top Hospital for superior outcomes, patient safety, and operational and financial performance. PVH and Medical Center of the Rockies (MCR) patient satisfaction scores surpassed the national top 10 percent, according to the Centers for Medicare and Medicaid Services. Dr. Rulon Stacey, former CEO of PVH, is vocal in his belief that these results are inextricably linked with the high levels of workforce engagement.

In 2008 when it received the award, the system's overall staff voluntary turnover rate decreased to 8 percent, well below that of competitors, and reached the Healthcare Human Resources Administration's top 10 percent performance level. The system's overall employee satisfaction ranked at the ninety-seventh percentile nationally, and *Modern Healthcare* magazine named PVH as one of "America's 100 Best Places to Work in Healthcare" in 2008.

In Figure 12.8, we see that the organization's voluntary turnover rate continues to be well below the benchmark from the American Society of Healthcare Human Resources Administration. Also in this figure are some of the human resource initiatives the organization put in place over time to continue to engage its workforce.

Hill Country Memorial (HCM)

Employee satisfaction and engagement scores, as well as those for employed and independent physicians, ranked HCM in the top 10 percent nationally for 2013 and 2014. HCM's voluntary employee turnover numbers have compared favorably to the top 25 percent of hospitals nationally as HCM has maintained a low turnover rate (compared to external benchmarks) for the past three years.

A highly engaged workforce has delivered exceptional care as demonstrated by these results:

- One of Top 100 Hospitals by Truven Health Analytics for 2012–2014.
- Top 10 percent nationally from Healthgrades for patient safety, general surgery, gastrointestinal care, and joint replacement.
- Outperformed every other hospital in Texas value-based purchasing and fifty-seventh of 3,200 hospitals nationally.
- HCM ranks consistently in the top 10 percent nationally on CMS clinical process measures, health care outcomes, and patient experience measures.

- Top 10 percent nationally for patient experience measures such as "overall rating of hospital," "communication about medications," "pain management," and "responsiveness of hospital staff."
- Restore Joint Center ranked HCM number one in 2013 for patient experience among 5,000 hospitals nationally.

At the same time, HCM demonstrated significant improvements in its financial performance from 2010 to 2013. During that period, HCM's net income increased from $10 million to nearly $20 million, cash flow to total debt ratios improved from 50 to 60, and cash and investments to debt ratios improved from less than 1.5 to higher than 3.

The organization also demonstrates positive trends in workforce productivity, as shown in Figure 12.9.

A similar increase in productivity is shown by the previously referenced Pewaukee School District in Figure 12.10.

FIGURE 12.9 Workforce Productivity, Hill Country Memorial

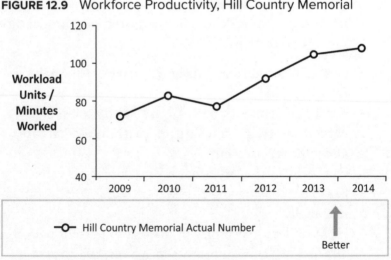

FIGURE 12.10   Productivity, Pewaukee School District

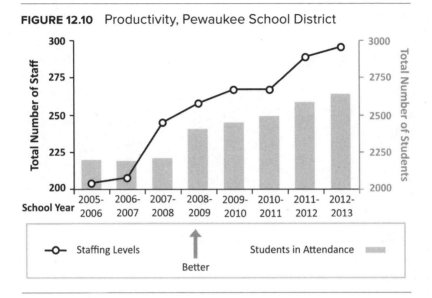

K&N Management

When this organization received the award in 2010, K&N demonstrated the effectiveness of its workforce engagement processes with turnover rates lower than industry averages for all categories of workers. For example, K&N Management's turnover rate for production workers was less than 50 percent, in contrast to the industry average of 85 percent. K&N Management's absentee rate was slightly more than 1 percent, compared to 5 percent for the best competitor and 3.5 percent for benchmarked organizations.

Over 95 percent of K&N Management team members reported they were proud to work for the company. In 2010, the *Austin American-Statesman* named K&N Management "the best place to work in Austin."

These engaged employees deliver outstanding customer service that produce enviable financial results. In sales, K&N Management's restaurants significantly outperform local competitors and national chains. The Rudy's "Country Store"

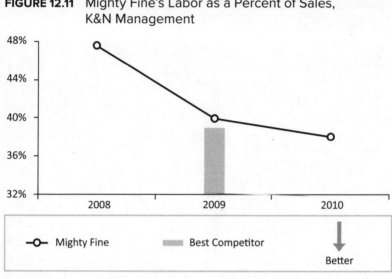

FIGURE 12.11 Mighty Fine's Labor as a Percent of Sales, K&N Management

& Bar-B-Q restaurants increased average unit sales from just over $3 million in 2000 to slightly more than $7.5 million in 2010 (for food sales only). From its inception in 2007 through 2010, Mighty Fine Burgers, Fries and Shakes increased annual unit sales from just over $2 million to more than $3.5 million in 2010, triple the unit sales of its best competitor.

Two measures of superior financial performance by K&N Management are shown in Figure 12.11 and Figure 12.12.

Another example of outstanding financial performance correlated with workforce engagement over time is demonstrated by MESA Products, Inc. in Figure 12.13. The dramatic increase in revenue is shown along with key milestones on the company's journey to performance excellence.

FIGURE 12.12   Rudy's Gross Profit, K&N Management

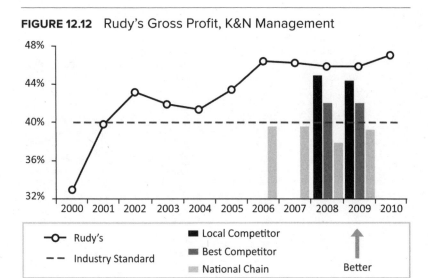

FIGURE 12.13   Growth History with Significant Milestones, MESA Products

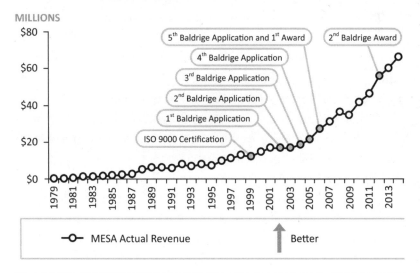

FIGURE 12.14 Correlation of Employee Engagement to Results, Park Place Lexus

		2010	2011	2012	2013	2014
PEOPLE	Member Retention – Percentage above Industry Benchmark	NA	NA	14.09%	11.60%	10.68%
	Number of Training Hours per Member	143.6	116.9	157.0	184.8	194.8
SERVICE	Service – Overall Client Engagement:					
	Park Place Lexus	**89.1%**	**88.9%**	**90.3%**	**91.8%**	**94.8%**
	National Lexus	86.0%	86.5%	87.5%	87.5%	93.7%
CLIENTS	Sales – Overall Client Engagement:					
	Park Place Lexus	**97.0%**	**96.9%**	**97.9%**	**97.6%**	**98.0%**
	National Lexus	95.4%	95.5%	95.4%	95.3%	96.5%
FINANCIAL	Total Revenue – Percentage Increase over Prior Year	12.01%	-1.30%	22.30%	6.60%	9.44%

Park Place Lexus (PPL)

In 2005 when the organization received the Baldrige Award, PPL ranked among the country's top Lexus dealers. Between 2000 and 2004, the company's gross profit increased by 51.3 percent. PPL members (employees) generated $387 million in revenue. In 2004, Park Place Lexus Grapevine's New Car Client Satisfaction Index (CSI) of 99.8 percent made it the highest-rated Lexus dealership in the nation.

What we see in Figure 12.14 is that PPL has continued its high level of employee engagement along with superior results for client engagement in sales and service—*and* financial performance.

In recent conversations with Ken Schnitzer, chairman of Park Place Dealerships (the parent organization of Park Place Lexus), he told us, "With an engaged workforce, you have higher customer satisfaction and more productivity. Our dealerships have some of the highest customer satisfaction in our industry. Our efficient operations benefit our customers and help the bottom line. Our turnover is 40 percent of the industry average, which provides for a more consistent customer experience and the cost savings resulting from not having to keep training new team members."

North Mississippi Medical Center (NMMC)

This two-time Baldrige Award recipient (first in 2006 and then again in 2012) demonstrates high levels of employee engagement along with corresponding high levels of performance in other areas of a balanced scorecard: service (patient satisfaction), quality (evidence-based care), financial, and growth. In Figure 12.15, it's clear that NMMC did not rest on its laurels after winning the Baldrige Award in 2006.

FIGURE 12.15 Correlation of Employee Engagement to Results, North Mississippi Medical Center

		2006	2007	2008	2009	2010	2011	2012
PEOPLE	Actively Engaged Employees Actual Percentage	30%		36%		40%		42%
	Actively Engaged Employees National Percentile	80th		98th		93rd		96th
	Overall Job Satisfaction National Percentile	88th		91st		98th		99th
SERVICE	Weighted Patient Satisfaction National Percentile		81st	92nd	93rd	93rd	91st	91st
QUALITY	Evidence Based Care National Percentile			90th	89th	95th	98th	
FINANCIAL	Bond Rating	AA	AA	AA	AA	AA	AA	AA
GROWTH	Inpatient Market Share in Service Area Percentage	40.5%	40.8%	41.5%	41.3%	40.7%	40.7%	NA

Summary

These are just a few of the many examples that Baldrige Award recipients can provide demonstrating what their senior leaders know. Aligning the workforce in accomplishing the mission of an organization and engaging employees in achieving the vision aren't just about having happy employees. Finding meaningful ways to engage employees' hearts, minds, and hands in the work of an organization delivers exceptional results that provide a competitive advantage in any industry or sector.

Employee Engagement and the Bottom Line—Checklist

1. How does your employee safety performance compare with that of your industry? If you're in health care, how does your patient safety compare with top quartile or top decile performance?
2. How many new jobs has your organization created in the past year?
3. How has your profitability grown over the past few years?
4. What results from this chapter were most compelling for you? Why?

Common Characteristics of the Leaders of Baldrige Award-Winning Organizations

- Focused on continuous improvement and valuing feedback
- Perseverance
- Personal involvement and serving as role models in all aspects of the journey
- Confident leadership with a little humility thrown in

At times during the interviews with leaders of Baldrige Award-winning organizations, we had a sense of déjà vu. Some of the responses were nearly identical despite differences in the organizations' size and sector, or the length of their journey. Many award winners said that being a recipient wasn't really the focus of their journey. It may seem that it is easy for leaders to say this when they have already won the award. However, the sincerity that we heard and the examples they gave of progress throughout the journey in transforming their organizations have convinced us that it truly was about the journey. Proof of this for us are the seven organizations that have won the Baldrige Award twice! You'll get insights from two of those leaders in the following section.

Focused on Continuous Improvement and Valuing Feedback

We asked Terry May, founder and CEO of MESA Products, Inc. (a Baldrige Award small business recipient in 2006 and 2012), why he reapplied for the award after winning his first one. He said, "We had grown tremendously, doubled in revenue and number of employees. In 2012, only 25 percent of the current workforce had been with us in 2006. I decided to apply again in 2012 because I thought during this growth cycle, we had relaxed and gotten a little lazy. For me, this was a checkup to see where we were and what needed to be worked on. And honestly, I thought maybe we shouldn't accept the award because we'll miss the opportunity to get another feedback report [the following year]." (But they did accept the award!)

Larry Potterfield, founder and CEO of MidwayUSA (Baldrige Award small business award recipient in 2009 and 2015), likes the challenge of proving that his organization is even stronger and more effective than when it won the first award. Since 2009, he and the president, Matt Fleming, and the other senior leaders have conscientiously worked to develop the team of middle managers to deepen their understanding of the Baldrige framework and their ability to lead using its principles. So confident were they in this leadership development that Matt and Larry delegated the interviews during the Missouri Quality Award site visit in 2015 to their middle managers. Other than the opening meeting, the senior leaders did not participate in the examiners' interviews. And yes, MidwayUSA won the Missouri Quality Award again in 2015 after first winning it in 2008.

Paul Worstell, retired CEO of PRO-TEC Coating Company (a Baldrige Award small business recipient in 2007), said, "The OFIs [Opportunities for Improvement] in the feedback report identify blind spots. We were very defensive at first, particularly about what we considered was our strategic planning process. The examiners kept telling us we weren't doing strategic planning." Ultimately, Paul and the senior leaders agreed. "We were creating an annual business plan and then putting it on a shelf. Mission statement—heck, we didn't even know where it was. In the early days, we didn't listen to the feedback. If we had listened, we would have accelerated our progress."

Dr. JoAnn Sternke, superintendent of the Pewaukee School District (a Baldrige Award education recipient in 2013), was always focused on continuous improvement. She admits that before the organization started on its Baldrige journey, "I was like a child hitting a piñata. That's how I approached improvement as a leader—just flailing. Before I started using the Baldrige framework, I was known for Random Acts of Cool Ideas."

Using the Baldrige framework allowed her to be more disciplined. "Sometimes that means taking things off the plate and saying no to things. It made me a better leader." She credits some of that to the feedback the organization received from its applications. "I became addicted to the feedback. The feedback was always part of the learning agenda for the board of education. We got more value from the feedback reports than what we received from our accreditation body."

JoAnn believes so strongly in helping others on the journey that she has posted the school district's applications and feedback reports on its website. She says, "In education, it's all about learning and sharing. A rising tide raises all ships. We want to make education better all across the country."

Harry Zechman, COO of Stoner, Inc. (a Baldrige Award small business recipient in 2003), said that his organization had been on a quality journey since the early 1990s. It was part of the company culture. Harry said, "We wanted to improve the business using a world-class, process-based leadership system. I was aware of the Baldrige Award from the

Reagan administration and had followed the early winners, Ritz-Carlton and FedEx. We had a mini-Baldrige program sponsored by our local Chamber of Commerce, which is how we got started."

At the 2015 Baldrige Quest for Excellence® Conference, Jayne Pope, CEO of Hill Country Memorial (a Baldrige Award health care recipient in 2014), shocked the audience when she said, "I am glad we did not win last year. The feedback was instrumental in getting better. The one thing I will miss is getting that feedback report."

Sister Mary Jean Ryan, FSM, former president and CEO, SSM Health Care (the first Baldrige Award recipient in health care in 2002), describes the value the organization has gotten out of the Baldrige process and the feedback it received. "Baldrige has offered us a way to systematically evaluate our entire organization and understand the link between the hundreds of processes that make up the health care experience. . . . Based on our Baldrige feedback, we've figured out how to deploy a consistent message throughout our organization. Our HR goals are now part of our strategic plan. We have developed a complaint management process that is used system-wide. We now benchmark against the highest-performing companies, whether or not they're in health care."

Dr. Bruce Kintz, president and CEO, Concordia Publishing House (a 2011 Baldrige Award recipient in the nonprofit category), credits the feedback his organization received with helping it thrive in challenging times, "In the past few years, we have seen a complete transformation of the book publishing industry. Despite this challenging landscape with the rapid-fire addition of new channels and business models, Concordia Publishing House continues to thrive. Our agility and flexibility during these times is due in great part to the guidance of the Malcolm Baldrige Criteria and the invaluable feedback from the examiners."

Dr. Joseph A. Lannon, the retired director of ARDEC (a Baldrige Award recipient in the government category in 2007), describes the approach his organization took to the journey. "The advantage of applying for these awards is not to win them or to receive them. It's to get the feedback from these experts from the outside who look at your organization in great detail and tell you what you do well and what you don't do so well. And we concentrated on the things that we didn't do so well to improve in those various areas."[1]

Allison Carter, director at PricewaterhouseCoopers Public Sector Practice (a 2014 Baldrige Award recipient), has said, "Your first instinct when you get the feedback report is to argue. But once you get past that initial defensiveness, and you really dig into the feedback, you recognize that there always is room for improvement. Our system was working great; our satisfaction scores were good. For our purposes, it was working well, and we didn't need to change it. But by using Baldrige and the other data that we pulled together, we were able to take a critical look at our processes and not just accept the status quo."[2]

Brian Dieter, president and CEO of Mary Greeley Medical Center (a 2014 recipient of the Gold Award by the Iowa Recognition for Performance Excellence), talked about how sometimes it was discouraging reading the feedback, but then he described a picture he had seen of a lion that was not successful with its hunt. The caption read, "I never lose. I either win, or I learn." Brian added, "If you go in with the right mindset, you will find truth in the feedback, and you will get better. That really fits with what I want to do with this organization. I don't want there to be a finish."

The first year the organization was eligible to apply for the Baldrige Award, it did. Brian explained, "Stay the course. If you're committed to improvement, then you're committed to improvement, not chasing a prize. We're not going to get another feedback report from our state program, so we had to apply to Baldrige."

Maryruth Butler, executive director of Kindred Nursing and Rehabilitation—Mountain Valley (a Gold Award recipient of the AHC/NCAL Quality Award Program in 2011), describes the feedback her organization received along the journey as "free industry consultation. Really look at the Opportunities for Improvement (OFIs) as a gift that will help your organization get better." Her advice for other organizations considering starting their own journey to performance excellence? "Just do it. Start on the journey. Once you start it, it won't be long before you realize the benefits. Responding to the Criteria will make you, as a leader, and your organization better."

Maureen Carland, administrator of the Maine Veterans' Home—Scarborough (AHCA Gold Award recipient in 2016), has the same advice. She says, "You'll never be 'ready' if you never start the journey. Start learning the Criteria. Start working with people who understand it."

Perseverance

In a recent interview, author Jim Collins commented, "One of the things that always struck me about the Baldrige process is it's a way of institutionalizing a culture of discipline. We're talking about making an entire cultural ethos where everyone is engaged in a systematic, methodical, consistent approach to making things work better day upon day, week upon week, year upon year, over a long period of time."[3]

Ken Schnitzer, chairman of Park Place Dealerships (parent company of Park Place Lexus, Baldrige Award recipient in the small business category in 2005), stated that he believed the reason that more leaders don't embrace Baldrige is because they look at it as extra work or extra cost. "They don't see the benefits. It takes a real commitment and a real effort. If you're focused on short-term results and not willing to put in the effort, it *will* be a waste of time and money. However, if you do the right things, it will be very rewarding."

This discipline is evident in most of the senior leaders we interviewed. Terry May shared that it took his organization five applications before it won its first Baldrige Award, but by that time "we were seeing some pretty dramatic improvement in our results."

Dr. JoAnn Sternke calls it persistence. "The idea of sticking with it—it's not about one and done. We submitted our first application to our state's program in 2007 and weren't a national recipient until 2013."

Dr. Bruce Kintz, CEO of Concordia Publishing House (a Baldrige Award nonprofit recipient in 2011), talked about the organization submitting its first application in 2003 to the Missouri state program. It continued to submit applications and won the state's highest level award in 2009. It won the Baldrige Award in 2011. When asked if he would do it again, Bruce replied, "Definitely yes. It was so much fun to see people's lightbulbs go on. There were so many blessings to watch people come along with it."

Karen Kiel Rosser, vice president and quality officer for Mary Greeley Medical Center, calls it "stick-to-itiveness." Echoing the sentiments of her boss, Brian Dieter, she said, "Commit to the time, and be in it for the long haul. Look at your feedback reports to see how much opportunity you still have."

Personal Involvement and Serving as Role Models in All Aspects of the Journey

In their bestselling book *The Leadership Challenge* (now in its fifth edition), James Kouzes and Barry Posner identified the five practices of exemplary leadership. The first of those is "Model the way." They explain that "Leaders' deeds are far more important than their words when constituents want to determine how serious leaders really are about what they say."[4]

Scott McIntyre, managing partner, PricewaterhouseCoopers Public Sector Practice, observed, "One thing that is patently obvious is that the senior leader of the organization has to be actively participating. How can this be genuinely achieved and be incorporated into your strategy if it isn't driven from the top? And the leader really needs to ensure that his or her actions are in line with the vision and values of the organization."

Ken Schiller, co-owner and cofounder of K&N Management (a Baldrige Award small business recipient in 2010), agrees. "Leadership has to come from the very top. I'm not delegating it. I'm accountable and lead by example, and then I can expect the same from everybody else."

Dr. David Spong the retired leader of two Boeing divisions that received the Baldrige Award (Boeing Mobility—formerly Airlift & Tanker [A&T] in the manufacturing category in 1998 and Boeing Support Systems—formerly Aerospace Support in the service category in 2003), frequently speaks about how Baldrige differs from Six Sigma, Lean, or other improvement approaches, although Boeing also uses those. He explains that most of those initiatives are managed by a program office that is separate from the normal chain of command for running the business. "Essentially, the leadership of the initiative can be delegated. That's just not possible with Baldrige. The senior-most executive will certainly have other people as change agents, as I had with Debbie Collard. But the senior leader has to be visible, relentless in communicating, and personally committed to the success of the journey."

Joan Brennan, vice president of quality and performance at AtlantiCare (a 2009 Baldrige Award health care recipient), talked about the value of David Tilton's personal leadership as president and CEO in their journey. She jokingly calls him *her* chief quality officer. Joan said, "If the CEO isn't committed to the journey and leading the effort, it's an exercise in futility." David quickly pointed out that it takes the whole senior leadership team. He said, "You lead the effort as a team. I benefitted from how the other senior leaders pushed me."

Pete Reicks, senior VP of performance excellence at Elevations Credit Union (a 2014 Baldrige Award recipient), said, "The Baldrige journey increased our capabilities as an organization and accelerated our ability to learn, improve, and innovate. We are continuing the journey, continuing to embrace the support provided by the Baldrige community, and have every intention to hopefully seek a Baldrige Award again."[5]

Confident Leadership with a Little Humility Thrown In

Terry May said, "We're very proud of what we've accomplished. There's a fine line between pride and ego, but when we compare ourselves to our competition, we think we're better. But we work hard to be humble."

Quint Studer, founder of the Studer Group (a Baldrige Award small business recipient in 2010), talked about the value in helping employees see that, "We're doing it to become a better organization. If we do those things, we'll earn—not win—the Baldrige Award."

JoAnn Sternke admitted, "We were very surprised when we received the award; we know how much better we can do. The journey continues."

Tommy Gonzalez, former city manager of the City of Irving (a Baldrige Award government recipient in 2012), describes undertaking the Baldrige journey in a highly political environment as challenging. "Through our application(s) and listening to our customers and stakeholders, we had to acknowledge all of the things we weren't doing very well. It's a humbling process. You're forced to make improvements because you've exposed yourself. That's not easy for prideful organizations."

Scott McIntyre, managing partner, PricewaterhouseCoopers Public Sector Practice (a Baldrige Award service recipient in 2014), said in response to a question at the Leadership Panel at the Quest for Excellence® Conference, "Baldrige was part of our vision, so we needed to provide the tools and invest in it with the commitment of our time. We had to set our egos aside. Look in the mirror and ask, 'What can we do better?'"

Jayne Pope described Hill Country Memorial's journey when it began using the Baldrige framework in 2007. When the organization compared its performance with top hospitals, "We weren't great. We needed a framework to get better, and we chose the Baldrige framework. And year after year, we got better until now we're in the top 1 percent in the nation." However, like so many other Baldrige Award recipients, Jayne acknowledged that the journey is never over. "We're not perfect. We have opportunities to learn. We can't linger. Our real work is ahead."

Pete Reicks of Elevations Credit Union also said in an interview with the Baldrige Program, "While we are proud of our Baldrige Award recipient status, the journey has also brought great humility. Our awareness and understanding of what world-class performance excellence truly looks like and how it applies to our situation is dramatically different than when we started the journey."

Common Characteristics of the Leaders of Baldrige Award–Winning Organizations—Checklist

1. Does your organization have a culture of continuous improvement? How do you foster that?
2. Where do you get objective feedback about how your organization is performing?
3. How do you identify the strengths and opportunities for your organization?
4. What would you need to do to personally lead a journey to performance excellence?

Lessons Learned
About the Journey

- The value of being an examiner and having others in the organization become examiners
- The value of the state/regional programs
- Not taking a year off
- It's not about the award; it's about the journey
- No more Baldrige "on the side"

In our interviews with leaders of Baldrige Award-winning organizations, we often asked, if they were to undertake the journey again in a different organization, what three things would they do differently, and what three things would they replicate? Their responses provided the insights in this chapter.

The Value of Being an Examiner and Having Others in the Organization Become Examiners

On April 2, 2015, a press release announced that for the second year in a row, the Baldrige Performance Excellence Program (BPEP) had received the first place award in the government and military category of the Leadership 500

Excellence Award, an annual recognition of the world's best leadership development programs and initiatives. Since 2010, BPEP has placed four times in the top 10 of this prestigious recognition. Examiners frequently talk about the value they have gleaned from their experience and often place it higher than an MBA. We both certainly feel that way.

Terry May, founder and CEO of MESA Products, Inc. (a Baldrige Award small business recipient in 2006 and 2012), started in the third year of the journey getting people trained as examiners for his state's program. "I was a national examiner in our fifth year. I should have been the first guy to go. It's the best way to learn the process. If I had done it earlier, I would have been able to calibrate things much quicker. Business owners need to be examiners at least once. I was on a site visit and benefited from seeing what other people in another organization did. The time commitment is hard, but the learning experience was wonderful."

Gerry Agnes, CEO of Elevations Credit Union (a Baldrige Award nonprofit recipient in 2014), said that in the beginning, no one in his organization was an examiner. Then a handful of people became examiners with the state program in the first two years. The organization now has about a dozen experienced state examiners and one examiner with the national program. Gerry says, "It helped to build the knowledge inside the organization that helped us along the journey."

Paul Worstell, retired CEO of PRO-TEC Coating Company (a Baldrige Award small business recipient in 2007), said that his organization's leaders got very involved in their state's program. They had employees get trained as examiners in the program. "That really accelerated things. It was a very, very effective way to move the organization forward at a more rapid pace."

Dr. JoAnn Sternke, superintendent of the Pewaukee School District (a Baldrige Award recipient in 2013), has shared that one of the ways the district accelerated its progress was having all of the senior leaders—as a team—become examiners, initially with their state program, and later some moved on to the national level. "It allowed us to speak the same language and develop our understanding of Baldrige together."

Diane Brockmeier, CEO of Mid-America Transplant Services (a 2015 Baldrige Award recipient), told us that beginning in 2007, the organization made it a requirement that all senior leaders had to become state or national examiners as part of their development. If someone is promoted into a senior leadership role, that person has to become an examiner within a year. "The best way to learn the Criteria is to review applications," she says. She also has valued her own experience as a national examiner since 2008. "I meet people I would otherwise never have met. I have great contacts across other industries. The Baldrige community is a generous one, sharing time and ideas."

When we asked Brian Dieter, president and CEO of Mary Greeley Medical Center (a 2014 recipient of the Gold Award by the Iowa Recognition for Performance Excellence), what he would do differently, he immediately said, "I'd have more examiners in the early years. The investment in developing examiners has paid off incredibly. The examiner skill set is invaluable to the organization. They bring back so much, and they serve as a catalyst for engaging the troops. It's also important for the CEO to demonstrate his commitment by supporting people from his organization in becoming examiners."

Probably no other senior leader has demonstrated his commitment and firm belief in the value of training employees as examiners more than Larry Potterfield, founder and CEO of MidwayUSA, a Baldrige Award small business recipient in 2009 and 2015. His first two examiners like to joke that they were "volun-told" about the opportunity to become an examiner. Since that first year, senior leaders have selected 10 to 15 high-potential employees to serve as examiners at either the state or national level. More than 35 percent of the salaried workforce are currently serving or have served as examiners for at least two years.

Matt Fleming, president of the organization, has stated, "I can't think of a better low-cost leadership development opportunity than sending your people to your state program or the national program to become examiners."

"I absolutely love this process," says Jake Dablemont, MidwayUSA's HR manager. "If I look at the value of what I've learned in grad school versus what I've learned as an examiner, I would choose to be an examiner every day of the week."[1]

Another employee chimed in, "It's a huge time commitment, but after you've done it for two years, you have a systems perspective. I could not have gone through a better leadership development program. After the training and going on site visits, it makes you slow down and ask why we are doing something. It's one thing to do something and get results, but it's another to know *why* you're getting the results."

The Value of the State/Regional Programs

Brenda Grant, chief strategy officer at Charleston Area Medical Center (CAMC) (a 2015 Baldrige Award recipient), shared that when her organization began its journey, West Virginia didn't have a Baldrige-based state or regional program. She said, "We just jumped right in with the national program. If we would have had a state program in the beginning, we wouldn't have stumbled as much as we did." Once the Ohio program expanded to include Indiana and West Virginia, CAMC applied twice to The Partnership for Excellence (TPE). "It was a great way to get more people engaged by becoming examiners, taking people to the annual TPE conference to learn from others on the journey. The regional program helped us accelerate our progress. And going through a site visit with the regional program was extremely helpful in preparing us for the national site visit." Since winning the TPE Platinum Award (the highest level), Brenda has served as a judge, and Dr. Glenn Crotty, CAMC's COO, serves on the board of trustees.

Terry May is also a strong proponent of starting with the state program, and he echoed Brenda's observation. He said, "It's much lower stress, particularly on the site visit." Terry is the past chairman of the board for Oklahoma Quality.

Gerry Agnes also started the journey with his state's program. "The state program was an absolutely integral part of our success. It helped us immensely. No one on our staff had any familiarity with Baldrige except one person who had been with FedEx [an early winner of the Baldrige Award in 1990]."

Dr. Mike Sather, former director of the Veterans Affairs Cooperative Studies Program Clinical Research Pharmacy Coordinating Center (a Baldrige Award government recipient in 2009), described going through all three levels of his state's program. Then the organization began applying for the Carey Award (a Baldrige-based program for Veterans Affairs that has subsequently been discontinued). Mike said, "The Carey Award was so important to us because the Carey Program [was] all about the Veterans. The Carey Program made more organizations in government get interested. The government of Libya even came over for a visit to see our operation."

The challenge for David Spong, retired leader of two Boeing divisions to receive the Baldrige Award (Boeing Mobility—formerly Airlift & Tanker [A&T] in the manufacturing category in 1998 and Boeing Support Systems—formerly Aerospace Support in the service category in 2003), with taking the Boeing Support Systems division on the Baldrige journey was that it was a very large organization with more than 13,000 employees spread across eight major sites in six states. He, in turn, challenged all site leaders to begin applying for their state program's highest level award. When that had been accomplished, David said, "That integrated the whole organization and enabled us to apply at the national level as one business." David is currently the vice chair of the board for the California Council for Excellence.

Tommy Gonzalez, former city manager for the City of Irving (a Baldrige Award government recipient in 2012), started his organization on the Baldrige Award journey with an application to his state's program. "Getting a third-party review is really helpful in assessing your progress. We also became more knowledgeable about the Criteria. Very few people tie all of the seven categories together outside of the Criteria. Using the Criteria and their interconnection helped us identify the silos in our organization." Tommy's belief in the value of the state program is demonstrated by his commitment to serving on the program's board of directors.

Dr. Bruce Kintz, CEO of Concordia Publishing House (a Baldrige Award nonprofit recipient in 2011), talked about using the first application in 2003 submitted to the Missouri state program as a "test pattern." The organization continued to apply to get the feedback. He also asked someone in the organization to go to "Baldrige School," to become an examiner with the state program, to become their internal expert.

Dr. Rulon Stacey, former CEO of Poudre Valley Health System (a Baldrige Award recipient in 2008), gave strong kudos to his state's program. Unlike the national program that has more of an arm's length distance from applicants along the journey to avoid any perception of conflict of interest, the state programs often develop strong relationships with their applicants. "The state program gave us more personal and more meaningful feedback, especially in our early years. They'd give us feedback, and a month later we'd call and ask for help. They'd send people over and give us advice." Having the option of applying at both the state and national levels allowed the organization to get ongoing and continued feedback.

Not Taking a Year Off

Although some of the leaders we spoke with talked about taking a year off to take the emphasis off of the application and use the time to make improvements, most of the other leaders disagreed. Terry May advises organizations to apply year after year. "Taking a year off makes it so much easier to take two years off. And if there's a leadership change, which happens in a lot of organizations, you just need the application process to be part of an expected annual effort that maintains its momentum in the face of change."

Paul Worstell echoes that sentiment. "Never, ever take a year off. If you take a year off, all you're going to do is take a year off. By the time we received the Baldrige Award, we realized it's not about the trophy, it's all about the OFI [Opportunities for Improvement]. It's all about the value of the feedback report. That's why you don't take a year off, you miss that feedback."

Ken Schiller, cofounder and co-owner of K&N Management (a Baldrige Award small business recipient in 2010), agrees. "Once you get the momentum going, don't stop and have to restart it."

At the 2014 Quest for Excellence Conference®, Kevin Unger, president and CEO of Poudre Valley Health System (a Baldrige Award health care recipient in 2008), stated, "Our first application scored in Band 3. We took a year off to 'focus on improvements.' We applied the next year and scored in Band 2. So we obviously accomplished nothing when we took a year off."

Rulon Stacey, former CEO of Poudre Valley Health System, reacted to the typical argument he gets from other senior leaders about the need to take a year off. "They say, 'You get the feedback report in December, and the next application is due in May. How do I have time to get these improvements in place?' That's the wrong question; it means you're running your business on one track and doing Baldrige on a parallel track. The point is to make meaningful improvement whenever you identify it. Apply when you can, and get feedback."

Diane Brockmeier, CEO of Mid-America Transplant Services (a 2015 Baldrige Award recipient), reinforces this. "Never take a year off. That's a year when you don't receive feedback, and some of the feedback for us was so profound. The other reason not to take a year off is that you learn something every time you write an application. It creates a foundation for critical thinking."

Pam Stoyanoff, COO of Methodist Health System (a 2015 Quality Texas Award recipient), said, "It makes sense to keep going when you have the momentum. It's like when you get out of college; it makes sense to go right on to graduate school to get your masters. I waited seven years, and it was incredibly hard to get refocused. When you take a year off, it's easy to take two years off, and then who knows?"

It's Not About the Award; It's About the Journey

Quint Studer, founder of the Studer Group (a Baldrige Award small business recipient in 2010), says that it's important to communicate that "it's a guideline and framework to accomplish our outcomes. It's not to win the award; that's a fringe benefit."

Gerry Agnes says that although senior leaders announced to the employees that they would win the Malcolm Baldrige

National Quality Award as their BHAG (Big Hairy Audacious Goal), he was clear with the board of directors that it was not about the award. "It's the journey to excellence. It's the better way we run our business." In fact, he told the board, "It's very likely that we will not receive this award while I'm your CEO." However, he was committed to getting the organization started on the journey.

Dr. Katherine Gottlieb, CEO of Southcentral Foundation (a Baldrige Award health care recipient in 2011), began using the Criteria to build a better organization in 2004. She never expected to go for the award. She and her senior leaders found that the nonprescriptive nature of the Criteria worked very well with their creative approaches. "It gives you the room to still be yourselves. With every question, it just caused us to reflect and improve. Those people who like the creative way, we love it." However, she also observed that the Baldrige framework works equally well for people who like detail and structure.

Scott McIntyre, managing partner, PricewaterhouseCoopers Public Sector Practice (a Baldrige Award service recipient in 2014), said the organization's approach was, "Let's win Baldrige by dramatically improving our business." Rick Rodman, a partner at the firm, continued, "This, for us, turned into a journey. Initially it was an application process, but then we started to understand the feedback. OFIs, cycles of refinement, and site visits." Scott continues, "You have to make sure that the leader and the team and the other constituents recognize that it *is* a journey, that it never ends regardless of the accolades. Also, a journey takes time. You need to give people time to innovate and fail. You have to have a mentality that says it isn't an overnight success story. As leaders, we have to be patient. And we have to acknowledge that continuous improvement is just that."

No More Baldrige "On the Side"

If you've ever seen the movie *When Harry Met Sally*, you'll understand this phrase. One of the main characters, Sally Albright, always ordered everything "on the side," so that she didn't have to commit to any condiments, sauces, or toppings. We see leaders in organizations that essentially have the same fear of committing to a performance excellence journey. As a result, Baldrige is done "on the side."

Rulon Stacey says, "If you make it about the award, people will think you're not serious about making improvement. We're on a continuous journey for improvement. You want to send that message at all costs. Make improvement all the time." He acknowledges that when Poudre Valley Health System began its journey, leaders managed it in "business as usual" mode until they started scrambling to prepare for their site visit. Feedback from one of their early site visits essentially said, "You say you do one thing, but it appears you really are running things a different way." They realized that operating on parallel tracks was putting too much stress on the system.

Rulon told the organization, "'We've either got to stop *doing* Baldrige, or we've got to *be* Baldrige.' We really started integrating the system. We had had seven category teams, but they operated in a vacuum. I suddenly realized that we had gotten worse. We'd created seven more silos in addition to who knew how many were already out there. Once we intentionally began to integrate those teams and share data and measures about the organization as a whole, we saw a huge inflection point in our results."

Dr. Steve Mansfield, CEO of Methodist Health System, talked about his "aha" moment when it clicked for him that "using the Baldrige framework for your performance excellence journey isn't another program. It's not another task. It's the very way you tackle your to-do list. The results of organizations using Baldrige are the best evidence out there as the approach to accomplish everything you are trying to do."

Lessons Learned About the Journey—Checklist

1. Do you have any examiners in your organization? Should you and your senior leaders become examiners to accelerate your own learning and enhance your performance as a team?
2. Are you familiar with your state or regional Baldrige-based program? Have you attended any of its conferences?
3. Have you contacted any of the award recipients from your state or regional Baldrige-based program to get insights from their leaders?
4. What will you do to maintain momentum on the journey?
5. How will you reinforce to the organization that it's about the journey and not the award?
6. How will you integrate your use of the Baldrige framework with the way you run your organization?

Other Benefits of Preparing an Application—Teamwork and Leadership Development

In addition to the valuable feedback that is received as a result of preparing and submitting an application, we have identified other benefits depending upon the approach an organization takes. As we worked with many clients over the years, we observed several different approaches that they took in preparing their applications. Some appointed a single writer whose task it was to interview others, solicit inputs, gather documents, and create each draft acting alone. Others developed category teams aligned with the categories of the Baldrige Criteria. And a few rare clients involved their entire senior leadership teams in developing their applications (although they may have had only one or two "writers" to provide a common voice throughout the application). This last approach was an enormous commitment of time on the senior leaders' parts, so we asked several clients why they chose this approach and whether they would recommend it to others.

The first client we asked was Maryruth Butler, executive director of Kindred Nursing and Rehabilitation—Mountain

Valley. To understand why this represented an enormous commitment, you need to understand this organization. It is a 68-bed long-term care facility in a very rural part of Idaho. (See the case study in Appendix B.) With only 90 employees working on three shifts, it's a very "flat" organization with not a lot of opportunity for the senior leaders to delegate their daily work. As we heard from others at very small organizations, part of the challenge is that the senior leaders wear multiple hats. Taking on the job of preparing the application adds to an already heavy workload.

When we asked Maryruth what the benefits were in engaging her senior leaders in this process, she was quick to explain. "Our team had been to multiple educational forums, but trying to understand the Criteria really changed our culture. We went from being very reactive to proactive. In the years before using the Baldrige framework, we had some good results because we got lucky. We didn't have systematic, repeatable processes to address problems and to prevent them. Then when we put processes in place, we asked ourselves if they were effective—and how did we know? Using data and graphs, we can now predict what is going to happen and change our actions if necessary."

As they worked through the different tiers of the AHCA/NCAL Quality Award program—Bronze, Silver, and Gold—they could tell from the feedback how they were improving. Maryruth continued, "When we began with the Quality Award program, becoming a Bronze recipient was a focus of the Kindred Healthcare corporation. However, we made the decision as senior leaders at the facility to commit to being excellent. Continuing along the journey was *our* decision. I'm very competitive, and along the way, I had to change my focus from the awards to helping our facility become 'Gold Award–worthy.'"

Three centers of the Maine Veterans' Homes (MVH)—Caribou (Melissa Graham), Machias (Marcia Jackson), and

Scarborough (Maureen Carland)—all took the same approach this past year in preparing their applications. We asked them to share some of their lessons learned working as entire senior leadership teams at each facility. Melissa jumped in saying, "We know it's a journey. If I'm taking the journey alone, I'm not going to excel and take the facility with me. Really, what good is it if it isn't a team approach? This approach shapes our culture." Marcia chimed in, adding, "We are such a team in Machias. No one does their job in a silo. We needed everybody there to tell the whole story. I wrote the Bronze application myself. It was a mistake. When we started to work on the Silver application together, nobody had any idea what I was talking about." Maureen responded, "I do not understand how you cannot involve all of the leaders. For all of us to be moving in the same direction, we all must speak the same language and all be moving toward the same goals. The team-building aspects of this approach to the journey cannot be overstated." MVH-Scarborough was named a Gold Award recipient in August 2016.

Deb Fournier, COO of Maine Veterans' Homes, who encourages all of the centers to undertake the journey to performance excellence, added her observations. "The commitment of professionals in the long-term care industry to get on this quality award journey is so very impressive because initially it does take additional time. As a whole, we are all very passionate about what we do for seniors. But I've seen how this process can be a mechanism to really build and solidify teamwork within a facility and how the process shifts our thinking from reactive to proactive." She added that she was not surprised the three MVH centers took the approach of involving the entire senior leadership teams. "Core to who we are as passionate leaders is our MVH values of 'excellence' and 'lead the way.' How could we not involve our teams? It's not sufficient for the one executive leader to do this work. Our commitment to hardwiring excellence demands involvement from all the leaders. As the COO, my goal is to create a sustainable culture of performance improvement where excellence permeates and is never ending. At MVH, we are all about exceeding the expectations of those we serve—our veterans."

When we spoke with David Tilton, CEO of AtlantiCare, about what approaches he would replicate if he led another organization on the journey to performance excellence, he quickly responded, "It all starts with the senior leadership team. If the CEO isn't surrounded by really capable, committed people, it isn't going to work. And developing the application together really helped solidify that teamwork."

We have encouraged our clients to also include "up-and-comers" in addition to senior leaders on the application preparation team. Pam Stoyanoff, COO of Methodist Health System, validated this approach. "We found unexpected benefits in pulling our application together. We assigned some high-potential middle managers to the effort and were able to see how they managed across functions and up and down the organization. They dealt so well with that and with the stress of a tight deadline. They also rose to the challenge of helping to manage the ad hoc interviews and requests that arose during our site visit, which required a lot of agility. One unexpected benefit was that we were able to see these high-potential middle managers demonstrate skills that will be so important as they rise up through the organization, and the other benefit for them is that they have a much more comprehensive view and knowledge of the whole system."

Other Benefits of Preparing an Application—Checklist

1. How could you involve your senior leaders in a performance excellence journey?
2. Who are some "high potentials" in your organization that would benefit from this leadership development experience?

Accelerating Excellence®

Sister Mary Jean Ryan, FSM, the former CEO of the first Baldrige Award recipient in health care (2002), SSM Health Care, has said, "I've always maintained that the reason to apply for Baldrige is that it's the best way to get better faster."[1] That's precisely what we mean by accelerating excellence®.

One of the areas that applying for Baldrige will cause you to reflect upon is your organizational culture. Is your culture accidental or intentional? Senior leaders of high-performing organizations act to create and sustain purposeful cultures designed to focus on excellence. Culture is a catalyst for accelerating excellence across a balanced scorecard. Increasing employee engagement is an essential strategy to accelerating excellence in an organization's performance. As we have shown earlier, increased employee engagement increases employee retention and bolsters productivity. Both help to increase the value provided to your customers. When this results in increased customer engagement and satisfaction, it fuels profitable growth, or—in the case of not-for-profit organizations—more revenue that can be used to further the mission.

We hope that the organizations featured in this book and their descriptions of their journeys have inspired you. But

FIGURE 16.1   Impact of Leadership Effectiveness on Employee Engagement

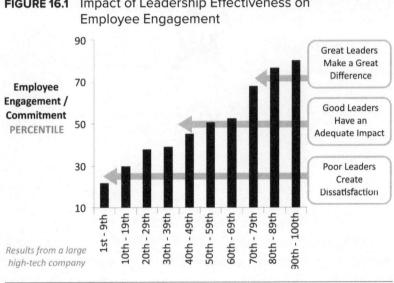

Results from a large high-tech company

inspiration is not sufficient; action is required. Your role as a senior leader cannot be overstated. The results found by Joe Folkman in the relationship between leadership effectiveness and employee engagement and commitment are shown in Figure 16.1.[2] The correlation between employee engagement and high performance have been demonstrated earlier in this book.

Although several leaders offered advice and lessons learned from how they started on this journey, your own leadership style and the prevailing culture of your organization will make your journey unique. However, we believe there are common first steps that are relevant for any organization.

First: The senior-most person in the organization must make a personal commitment to performance excellence. This will need to be reflected in your every action and every decision because all eyes of the organization will be focused on you, weighing the sincerity of your message to take the organization to higher levels of performance. You will need to continuously demonstrate your lack of tolerance for the status quo and your belief that the organization can achieve the lofty goals you describe. Using the examples from this book may help you convince skeptical employees that such performance is indeed possible.

Second: You will need to decide how you want to announce your decision. Most of the senior leaders we talked with emphasized the need to avoid launching the effort with a "big bang." Many cautioned against talking about the award, although a few used the achievement of the award as their BHAG (Big Hairy Audacious Goal) (Elevations Credit Union) or a way to differentiate themselves in a crowded market (PricewaterhouseCoopers Public Sector Practice). We have seen several organizations that "brand" their journey so that it is more meaningful to the employees and reinforces the notion that this is how everyone will be doing work going forward (MESA Products and the "Mesa Way").

Third: You will need to get your other senior leaders on board through some means, such as demonstrating the need for change or describing a compelling opportunity. However, if after some amount of time you have a senior leader who will not commit to the journey, you need to get that person off the bus. That may seem like a drastic action to take, but a resistant senior leader will undermine the forward movement of the rest of the organization. Passive resistance is sometimes even more toxic because it can cause you to doubt whether you are reading the signals correctly. Challenge the person to publicly voice his or her commitment and demonstrate it with results.

Fourth: You will get much better traction if you tie this journey to the higher purpose of your organization. Sister Mary

Jean Ryan, FSM, former CEO of SSM Health Care (the first Baldrige Award recipient in health care in 2002), has told her story at several of the conferences we've attended. SSM Health Care's journey started with implementing Continuous Quality Improvement (CQI) in 1990. As Sister Mary Jean describes it, she returned from a leadership conference where there had been multiple presentations on CQI. She and her regional vice president, Bill Thompson, discussed whether CQI, which had primarily been demonstrated in manufacturing, could be applicable in a health care setting. When they decided it could, Sister Mary Jean returned to the organization and announced to the board that SSM was going on a CQI journey. And she describes their reaction as something like, "Okay, knock yourself out, Sister." They thought CQI was a mechanical approach and unrelated to the higher purpose of the organization.

Sister Mary Jean explains, "In retrospect, I realize the comments of the Board pushed us to better define how CQI meshed with our values as an organization. That critical link became the foundational piece of our CQI educational material." And CQI became the starting point for what would become their "journey to move SSM Health Care from a little better than average to exceptional."[3]

We also heard from other senior leaders about the importance of reinforcing the organization's mission, vision, and values as the underpinnings of the performance excellence journey.

Fifth: Leverage existing improvement methodologies in your organization, whether they are PDCA, PDSA, Six Sigma, Lean, or some other approach that you have been using. However, if there isn't a common approach to process improvement in your organization, now is the time to select and implement one and ensure that everyone is trained in its use. Teams with a common language are able to more quickly and effectively come together to tackle problems and solve them.

There are two important types of early improvement projects. The first are projects tied directly to your strategic plan. If you can demonstrate that this journey helps deliver against important objectives, you will do a lot to gain the support of your board, customers, and other key stakeholders. The second type of early improvement projects are those that help make the jobs of front-line staff easier. A key role of senior leaders in any organization is removing barriers that get in the way of employees being able to do their jobs effectively and efficiently. When you begin to remove some of those barriers, you gain employee buy-in.

Sixth: Help the workforce (including collaborators and partners) understand how your organization is doing and how their jobs contribute to those results. Make sure that data are visible and that there is a line of sight between every employee and the highest level objectives of your organization. Develop data displays at the organizational unit level so that employees can track their own progress and take responsibility for addressing adverse trends.

Seventh: Seek out aggressive benchmarks. Choose sources of comparison from inside and outside of your industry. Seek top quartile and top decile performance rather than comparisons against averages. If all of your comparisons are against other units of your own company, you risk being only the best pig in a bad litter. Or to put it another way, Horst Schulze, former CEO of the Ritz-Carlton Hotel Company (a two-time Baldrige Award recipient in 1992 and 1999), related at a conference that once they started to compare themselves outside of just the hotel industry against the entire service sector, "We were the cream of the crap."

One of the biggest surprises most organizations and their employees have when they begin their journey comes from finally having the data to understand where their performance really measures up. In many cases, they are confronted with the realization that they are not as good as they believed they were. This is not a comfortable position for most of us with an inherently competitive spirit. Use this discomfort to accelerate the momentum for improvement in your organization.

Eighth: Demonstrate patience with a sense of urgency. Acknowledge that this is a journey and not a sprint. However, remain attentive to constantly moving the bar higher. It may be helpful to focus on your competitive environment to communicate the need for accelerated improvement.

Ninth: As we described in Chapter 4, one of the most powerful tools an organization can use to drive employee engagement is to measure it regularly. In addition, senior leaders must personally own the processes for analyzing the feedback, sharing it with the workforce, and then ensuring that issues are addressed—either resolved or a clear explanation given as to why something requested won't be put in place.

Tenth: Become personally knowledgeable regarding the Baldrige Excellence Framework, invest in developing internal expertise, and seek skilled experts and coaches who can help you understand the complex principles and language of the Criteria. Even professional athletes with innate talents rely on coaches to improve and accelerate their performance.

With the insights gleaned from leaders of Baldrige Award–winning organizations and those that have won awards from Baldrige-based programs, you have the ability to jump-start your own journey to performance excellence. Select two or three best practices that you can implement immediately as you begin to use the Baldrige Excellence Framework to improve your organization, engage your workforce, delight your customers, and achieve enviable results.

APPENDIX

A

Additional References and Resources

There are many resources readily available to satisfy your curiosity and support you as you explore what a performance excellence journey might mean to you and your organization.

The Baldrige Program Website
http://www.nist.gov/baldrige/

The Baldrige Foundation Website
http://www.baldrigepe.org/foundation/

The Alliance for Performance Excellence Website
You can find the Baldrige-based program that supports your state.
http://www.baldrigepe.org/alliance/

Baldrige Resource Library Hosted on Alliance for Performance Excellence's Website
http://www.baldrigepe.org/brl/

The American Health Care Association/National Center for Assisted Living (AHCA/NCAL) Quality Award Program Website
http://www.ahcancal.org/quality_improvement/quality_award/Pages/default.aspx

A Website Provided by MidwayUSA
This site contains links to white papers and presentations across each of the Baldrige categories.
   http://americaneedsbaldrige.com/

Pewaukee School District's Baldrige Journey
This site includes links to the Pewaukee School District's applications and feedback reports.
   http://wi-forwardbaldrige-quali.pewaukeeschools.schoolfusion.us
   /modules/groups/integrated_home.phtml?&gid=2959116&sessionid=
   43d8f469c991cfb40db9bbb63a44a955&_gat=1&_ga=GA1.2.2044
   119260.1436022784

Presentations and Videos by Elevations Credit Union at the 2015 Quest for Excellence Conference
   https://www.elevationscu.com/quest

Downloadable Business Process Workbook from Elevations Credit Union
   https://www.elevationscu.com/process

Downloadable eBook on Culture from Elevations Credit Union
   https://www.elevationscu.com/community/careers

Video About the PRO-TEC Coating Culture
   http://www.proteccoating.com/associates-video/

Video About K&N Management's Work Ethic
   https://www.youtube.com/watch?v=m6nPuWQ30y8

The Authors' Websites
   http://www.baldrigecoach.com/
   http://www.baldrigebooks.com
   http://www.bronze-to-silver.com
   http://www.silver-to-gold.com

Case Study: Unexpected Excellence at Kindred's Mountain Valley*

Tucked away in the Silver Valley of northern Idaho, in the small town of Kellogg, lies a jewel. Like a gemstone in a piece of costume jewelry, Kindred's Nursing and Rehabilitation—Mountain Valley (KNRMV) sparkles among the many long-term care and rehabilitation facilities across the country.

KNRMV provides long-term care and short-term rehabilitation services, with 68 licensed beds and a workforce of 90 employees and 23 key volunteers. If you read a fact sheet about it, it would sound much like any other facility offering those services. However, it manages to differentiate itself in multiple ways.

Mountain Valley had already won the American Health Care Association's (AHCA) Bronze and Silver Quality Awards. (The AHCA/NCAL Quality Awards are based on the Baldrige Criteria.) Maryruth Butler, the executive director, had submitted three applications for the Gold Award (AHCA's highest level award)—each unsuccessful. I (Kay) read them before heading out to Kellogg, Idaho, in the bitter winter of 2010

---

* This case study is based on an article originally published in the April 2012 issue of *The Journal for Quality and Participation.*

to meet with Maryruth and her team. To be truthful, my expectations were fairly low based on the applications, which described a fairly unremarkable organization.

My first pleasant surprise was how beautifully the lobby had been decorated in preparation for the holidays. Residents and staff were milling around the lobby with a quiet hum of conversations punctuated by occasional laughter. Then I met Maryruth and some members of her staff. During a lunch meeting to try to tease out what makes this organization unique, I was amazed at some of the stories I heard. These reflected the deep commitment the staff—at all levels, in all positions—have to the residents. I heard many examples—some humorous, some touching—of how the staff and volunteers go out of their way to make the lives of their residents better in very individualized ways.

The organization has that same palpable culture of continuous improvement that we see in Baldrige Award recipients. But what surprised me was that the workforce, including Maryruth, takes that as a "given," that all organizations must be like that. None of that dedication to excellence had come through in those previous three Gold Award applications. Now, many organizations are arrogant and believe themselves to be better than they really are. Here was an organization that truly did not understand the depth to which it demonstrates excellence across a variety of dimensions. I want to share a few of those.

Senior leaders at Mountain Valley personally serve as role models for the organization's values. Whether it is Maryruth taking a dessert cart to each resident once a week (demonstrating respect) or Emilee, the assistant director, serving to facilitate an improved relationship between an agitated resident and her mother (demonstrating excellence), the values are reinforced by the senior leaders' behaviors. A very real open-door process makes Maryruth available to the staff and volunteers and to the residents and to their families. In truth, many never even need to come through the open door of Maryruth's office. They freely express concerns, questions, and compliments as she makes her way on daily senior leader rounding through the facility. The personal relationships that she and the rest of the staff have with the residents can be seen in the many spontaneous hugs I witnessed while touring the facility.

Personalized care for the residents is evident in large and small ways. About 10 years ago, the staff determined that one resident was homesick for her garden, so they developed a raised bed garden, accessible from a wheelchair, with a patio. Since then, the garden has become the focus of a lot of activity for many of the residents during the growing season. The residents raise garlic and pick cherries, which they then sell to the staff to make a little extra spending money.

Another example of listening to the "voice of the customer" and creating an experience beyond expectations was the segmentation of various customer feedback data. Because the majority of residents are female, Maryruth decided to drill down more into the opinions of the male residents. While overall satisfaction and loyalty for both male and female residents had been nearly at the 100 percent mark on the customer satisfaction survey for several years, the male residents expressed some wishes during focus group meetings and one-on-one conversations. One of these wishes had to do with their sense that the decor of the facility was too feminine. Maryruth took that feedback and put together a plan to convert a space in the facility into a "man cave" with a regulation-size pool table, a big-screen television, a few recliners, and even a "bar" where male residents and volunteers could now socialize in their own space.

In 2015, in another cycle of improvement, the senior leaders assessed how their resident population had changed, and they realized that the pool table allowed only the more independent residents to play because of limited space in the room and the difficulty the residents had in getting around the table. Then the facility admitted a pleasant though confused lady and her husband together. However, the wife would never go in that room with him or to therapy because it was the "man cave," and she thought women were not allowed. The senior leaders solicited feedback through interviews at the resident council, through abaqis (a customer satisfaction survey tool), and during care conferences. The pool table was removed following a majority approval vote at a resident council meeting. A large flat-screen Smart TV was installed along with a bookcase with large print books. They added another table so that one empty table was available for residents to have meals with their families. With the second table, they can have a jigsaw puzzle always in progress and still have room for a board game. They renamed the "man cave" the TV Room.

In a subsequent cycle of evaluation and improvement, they learned that their residents still wanted some type of hands-on game, so the facility purchased a small game table that has foosball on one side and Ping-Pong on the other side. Since the room was no longer dominated by the TV, it was once again renamed to become the Rec Room. Maryruth still ensured that it is decorated in a neutral manner with no "girlie stuff." She just added iPads and a laptop in early March, and the residents *love* the room!

In order to expand opportunities for socializing, family members and visitors are encouraged to eat lunch with residents—at no cost! The facility currently serves daily lunches to seven spouses. Another innovative idea came from a collaboration with an adjacent K–6 school. The school had no property beyond its building, while Mountain Valley is centered on 3.3 acres. KNRMV offered space to the school for a large playground. This way, the residents could interact with the students during recess on each school day. Each Tuesday, the students came over and gave some kind of performance for the residents. Both students and residents loved the relationships that developed. In 2006, when the facility learned that the school did not have the funds to upgrade the playground equipment, it jointly sponsored a fund-raising initiative in the community to obtain the funds. In 2010, the Mountain Valley resident council voted to devote funds to again update the playground equipment to ensure the continuation of the positive engagement with the students.

However, in 2013, the school moved to another location, making it difficult for its students to access the playground on a regular basis. The resident council members reached out to a local daycare facility offering it the opportunity to use the playground equipment. Since then, the daycare has moved closer to the center supporting regular use of the playground equipment and providing the staff with convenient access to child care.

Despite its small size, Mountain Valley also demonstrates a focus on workforce engagement. A longstanding investment in the education and development of staff has resulted in strong succession planning, multiple examples of career progression, and an enviable level of long-tenured employees. The atmosphere at Mountain Valley serves as one of its recruiting tools. One of the nurses joined the organization after she witnessed the environment there when she was delivering a sandwich from a local delicatessen. There are many examples of relatives working at the facility, including one with three generations from one family.

The commitment to the community takes several forms. One of these includes taking in residents who were homeless. One example is "Bill," who was raised in the Silver Valley. In fact, he and his sister had lived in their family home. In 2008, his sister and her significant other were both admitted as residents to the center. Several senior leaders were contacted by community members who were worried about Bill and felt he wasn't eating well, wasn't taking care of himself, and had poor living arrangements. This information was communicated to the workforce and Emilee. They responded to the situation with exceptional customer service. Bill was not receptive to them "fussing" over him, and he tried to convince them he was fine. He is a very private man, but Emilee employed the help of Bill's sister and her significant other to convince Bill to have meals with them, creating a family atmosphere, like old times. Bill agreed and began eating meals there three times a day.

In December 2008, when winter hit the local area hard, community members again reported concerns about Bill's living arrangements. Bill had been limping for a few days. The senior leaders convinced him to see a physician, and he was a direct admission to the facility that day, secondary to multiple falls at home and possible frostbite as he had been living with no heat or water. Bill has since been named the Outstanding Resident of the Year at Mountain Valley every year from 2009 through 2015. In 2011, he was named the State of Idaho's Resident of the Year. He is currently participating in the center's succession planning for key volunteers. One of the community members who was key to communicating with senior leaders about Bill now has placed her mother at the center. She volunteers two nights a week to lead bingo with Bill.

In addition to strong, systematic processes and an organization with "heart," Mountain Valley demonstrates impressive results. In patient-focused outcomes such as pain management, pressure ulcers, mobility, and quality of life measures, Mountain Valley significantly outperforms its best competitor and national and State of Idaho averages. Most measures of resident and family satisfaction are at or near 100 percent. Overall employee turnover rates are around 20 percent, which compares with estimates of between 39 percent and 127 percent for this industry. Turnover in LPN positions has been zero percent since 2009 with RN turnover at zero percent four out of the six years. Results from employee satisfaction surveys show continued improvement trends. In 2015, 90 percent of Mountain Valley's employees agreed with the statement that they felt a sense of accomplishment in their work. Total volunteer hours in 2015 exceeded 14,000 hours!

The organization has received numerous recognitions, including the CMS Five-Star Overall Quality Rating in 2009 and every year thereafter. In 2010, it was among *U.S. News & World Report*'s "America's Best Nursing Homes"—the only facility in Idaho to be so named. And in 2011, it was named the only Gold Award recipient for the AHCA Quality Award.

In recognition of achieving the Gold Award, the Kindred Corporation presented Mountain Valley with a check for $100,000. As she had done with a smaller check for receiving the Silver Award, Maryruth immediately announced her commitment to "reinvest" the monies back into things that would improve the lives of residents. In 2007, the money was used to purchase a second van to increase access for the residents to specialty care appointments outside of the Silver Valley. In 2011, Maryruth used the money to upgrade sinks and cabinets in residents' rooms to make them handicap accessible as well as more attractive.

What inspires me about Mountain Valley's story is its commitment to achieving excellence in ways large and small on a daily basis. While other facilities exist in the Silver Valley area and in the larger Coeur d'Alene area, Mountain Valley is always full and has a standing waiting list. It has a similar waiting list for staff openings. Loyal customers and stakeholders, respect from the communities it serves, engaged employees and volunteers, and outstanding results are all hallmarks of an excellent organization and a leader who recognizes that it isn't about an award, it's about the ongoing journey to performance excellence.

APPENDIX

C

The Baldrige Award Process

- The application process—from the applicant's perspective
- The importance of confidentiality—from the examiners' and the applicant's perspectives
- The assessment process—from the examiners' perspective
- The site visit process—from the examiners' and the applicant's perspectives
- The evaluation and recommendation process—from the judges' perspective
- The award notification process—from the award recipient's perspective

Although some organizations use the Baldrige Excellence Framework as an internal assessment tool, obviously the organizations featured in this book have submitted applications to the national Baldrige Performance Excellence Program (BPEP) or other Baldrige-based programs. Some of these other programs offer tiered levels of awards with corresponding differences in the page limits at each tier. The assessment process, the site visit process, and the judges' process are based on the national program with some variation based on the program administrators' understanding of the customers they serve in their markets. Fees also differ from program to program with most providing a "break" for not-for-profit, education, and very small organizations.

FIGURE C.1   Baldrige Award Process Review Cycle

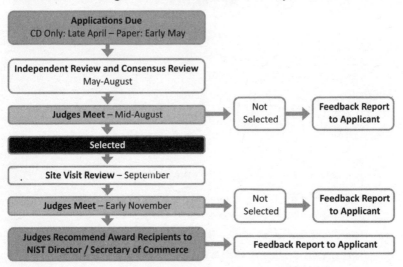

In this appendix, we are going to look at the award process review cycle for the national program, the "gold standard" for Baldrige. The Award Process Review Cycle is shown in Figure C.1.

The Application Process—from the Applicant's Perspective

"I know of nothing quite like the Baldrige application. It compels companies to go through a self-examination in seven categories. . . . It's not like any normal award for which you might have someone spend a couple of days filling out a 5- or 6-page application."[1] This is a description provided by the Xerox Corporation Business Products and Systems, which won the Baldrige Award in 1989. Most organizations form teams to develop their applications, usually over a period of several months. The nature of the questions in the Criteria require deep reflection and candid discussion among the senior leaders, even in very mature organizations. A Baldrige application is a detailed description of the key processes of an organization along with a data-dense part that provides evidence of the results across multiple areas of performance.

Most organizations will make their way to an application submitted to the national program after winning the highest-level award from another Baldrige-based program. However, BPEP does have a provision for organizations to bypass this step and submit directly to the national program provided they can meet the eligibility criteria. Complete information on how to apply for the Baldrige Award is available at http://www.nist.gov/baldrige/enter/how_to_apply.cfm.

One of the eligibility requirements relates to the length of time since an organization has previously won the Baldrige Award. Recipients are ineligible to reapply for the award for five years. Other eligibility requirements relate to the percent of employees located in the United States and whether the unit of a parent organization operates with sufficient autonomy with its own senior leaders and with the ability to provide responses for all of the categories. Submitting the eligibility form also serves as an organization's notice of its intent to apply (although it may drop out of the process if it chooses). This enables BPEP to anticipate the number of examiners it will need as well as the likely mix of sectors that the examiners will have applications to assess.

The Importance of Confidentiality—from the Examiners' and the Applicant's Perspectives

All examiners and judges sign a Code of Ethical Conduct regarding their professional behavior that reflects the high standards of the Baldrige Program. Examiners and judges also must disclose any potential conflicts of interest such as current or former employers, key customers, key suppliers, personal relationships with any organization's senior leaders, or significant financial holdings with any organization. BPEP assigns examiners to an application taking into account experience, sector knowledge, and freedom from any known conflicts of interest. However, examiners are still required to review the application upon its receipt and answer a list of questions to attest to their lack of conflicts of interest. In the case of any question, examiners contact BPEP for a decision.

Since its inception, the Baldrige Program has assured applicant organizations of the protection of their information and maintained secrecy about the applicants' identities. For example, examiners may never reveal to anyone—even other examiners not assigned to their team—the identity of any organization they have evaluated. They may never disclose any site visits on which they participated. Examiners are even required to return the applications to ASQ (American Society for Quality), the contracted administrator, for tallying and destruction. Organizations may choose to publicize that they have applied or received a site visit, but the examiners and BPEP consider that choice to be strictly the applicant's.

More information about the integrity of the Baldrige Process can be found at www.nist.gov/baldrige/about/process _integrity.cfm.

The Assessment Process—from the Examiners' Perspective

Baldrige examiners are selected based on comprehensive applications they submit that identify their educational background, work history, any Baldrige-related experience, and self-assessed capabilities in evaluating the seven Baldrige categories as well as skills in leadership, writing, teamwork, and so on. New examiner applicants must also provide two letters of reference. Being selected to be a Baldrige examiner is a high honor because of the rigorous selection process and degree of competition. There are generally four applications submitted for every examiner selected. Examiners and judges are all volunteers and receive no paid compensation for their contributions.

One benefit to applicants is that they may provide the name of someone in their organization who is guaranteed to be appointed to the Board of Examiners the year their application is submitted. We recommend that applicants take advantage of this opportunity by submitting the name of a senior leader or an identified high-potential middle manager for a powerful leadership development opportunity.

All examiners and judges, whether new or returning, must participate in examiner training. Before coming to training, they must complete prework using a case study. This prework generally takes between 12 and 20 hours. The case study is a key component of the examiner training experience and is developed by a small team of examiners to depict a fictional organization that exhibits some of the best practices and results reflective of a good organization in the assigned sector. The case study is reviewed by a team of subject matter experts, and then another team of experienced examiners performs their independent reviews and then consensus to provide a feedback report exactly like one that a real applicant would receive. Both the case study and its related feedback report serve as good examples to applicants. The most recent ones are available on the Baldrige website.

During examiner training, the examiners participate in highly interactive exercises using the Baldrige Criteria and the case study to develop comments—Strengths and Opportunities for Improvement (OFIs)—and assign scores to each item. This training helps the examiners deepen their understanding of the Criteria, calibrates the Board of Examiners on appropriate scoring, and begins to foreshadow the work that will occur during consensus.

Independent Review is exactly like what it sounds. Shortly after training, examiners receive their application, check for any conflicts of interest, and begin reading the application. Most examiners will read the application several times before they draft what are called Key Factors. This important step ensures that examiners focus on the uniqueness of the organization, which further helps them write comments that reflect what is most important to the applicant. After drafting the Key Factors, examiners—independently—begin to evaluate each item, draft comments, and assign scores. During this stage, none of the examiners have contact with each other besides the team leader who periodically checks in with examiners to ensure they are making progress against the agreed-upon milestones. Examiners typically spend between 20 and 40 hours at this stage depending on their experience and the complexity of the application. All work is done in a secure web-based application that is password protected. No applicant-specific information is shared via e-mail to protect confidentiality. In addition, the only information that can be used during the evaluation process is the application itself. Internet searches or review of an applicant's website are not permitted.

When all examiners have completed their Independent Reviews, their work is combined into a single document sorted by the Categories and Items of the Criteria. A lead and back-up examiner are assigned to each Category. They provide each other feedback and make revisions. After that has been completed, all Items are made available for the entire team to review, make comments, and revise prior to the consensus calls. Completion of the consensus process occurs over the course of two teleconferences. These typically last from four to six hours each.

During these calls, the examiners review each item, identify the most important comments—both Strengths and OFIs—and assign a score. The examiners also develop what are known as Key Themes, which are the most significant cross-cutting observations in both Strengths and OFIs for processes and results. These are sometimes referred to as "The Executive Summary." Then they do one final "sanity check," which is to review the tallied scores against the scoring bands that describe different levels of organizational maturity (Figure C.2).

If the judges select an applicant to move forward in the process, the examiners begin to prepare for a site visit.

The Site Visit Process—from the Examiners' and the Applicant's Perspectives

The team of examiners from consensus are likely to be the same examiners who will conduct the site visit. However, because of schedule conflicts or the need for more subject matter expertise, examiners who are new to the team may be added. The site visit team has two objectives: they clarify any OFIs (validate that they are true gaps in the organization rather than an artifact of the application itself) and verify Strengths that might serve as role model practices for other organizations.

In preparation for the site visit, examiners prepare site visit issue (SVI) worksheets that spell out specifically what must be verified or clarified, the related comments in the consensus report, and their plan for closing out the issue. This may include requesting and reviewing documentation during the site visit, formal interviews with senior leaders and other subject matter experts, and informal discussion with frontline employees using "walk-around questions." They will also request and review updated results from the time the application was submitted. The team leader coordinates the schedule with the applicant's Official Contact Point (OCP).

FIGURE C.2 Scoring Band Descriptors

Band Score	Band Number	PROCESS Descriptor	Band Score	Band Number	RESULTS Descriptor
0–150	1	The organization demonstrates early stages of developing and implementing approaches to the basic Criteria requirements, with deployment lagging and inhibiting progress. Improvement efforts are a combination of problem solving and an early general improvement orientation.	0–125	1	A few results are reported responsive to the basic Criteria requirements. These results generally lack trend and comparative data.
151–200	2	The organization demonstrates effective, systematic approaches generally responsive to the basic Criteria requirements, with some areas or work units in the early stages of deployment. The organization has developed a general improvement orientation that is forward-looking.	126–170	2	Results are reported for several areas responsive to the basic Criteria requirements and the accomplishment of the organization's mission. Some of these results demonstrate good performance levels. The use of comparative and trend data is in the early stages.
201–260	3	The organization demonstrates effective, systematic approaches responsive to the basic requirements of most Criteria items, with areas or work units still in the early stages of deployment. Key processes are beginning to be systematically evaluated and improved.	171–210	3	Results address areas of importance to the basic Criteria requirements and accomplishment of the organization's mission, with good performance being achieved. Comparative and trend data are available for some of these important results areas, and some trends are beneficial.
261–320	4	The organization demonstrates effective, systematic approaches generally responsive to the overall Criteria requirements. Deployment may vary in some areas or work units. Key processes benefit from fact-based evaluation and improvement, and approaches are being aligned with overall organizational needs.	211–255	4	Results address some key customer/stakeholder, market, and process requirements, and they demonstrate good relative performance against relevant comparisons. There are no patterns of adverse trends or poor performance in areas of importance to the overall Criteria requirements and the accomplishment of the organization's mission.
321–370	5	The organization demonstrates effective, systematic, well-deployed approaches responsive to the overall requirements of most Criteria items. The organization demonstrates a fact-based, systematic evaluation and improvement process and organizational learning, including innovation, that result in improving the effectiveness and efficiency of key processes.	256–300	5	Results address most key customer/stakeholder, market, and process requirements, and they demonstrate areas of strength against relevant comparisons and/or benchmarks. Improvement trends and/or good performance are reported for most areas of importance to the overall Criteria requirements and the accomplishment of the organization's mission.
371–430	6	The organization demonstrates refined approaches generally responsive to the multiple Criteria requirements. These approaches are characterized by the use of key measures, good deployment, and innovation in most areas. Organizational learning, including innovation and sharing of best practices, is a key management tool, and there is some integration of approaches with current and future organizational needs.	301–345	6	Results address most key customer/stakeholder, market, and process requirements, as well as many action plan requirements. Results demonstrate beneficial trends in most areas of importance to the Criteria requirements and the accomplishment of the organization's mission, and the organization is an industry* leader in some results areas.
431–480	7	The organization demonstrates refined approaches responsive to the multiple Criteria requirements. It also demonstrates innovation, excellent deployment, and good-to-excellent use of measures in most areas. There is good-to-excellent integration of approaches with organizational needs, with organizational analysis, learning through innovation, and sharing of best practices as key management strategies.	346–390	7	Results address most key customer/stakeholder, market, process, and action plan requirements. Results demonstrate excellent organizational performance levels and some industry* leadership. Results demonstrate sustained beneficial trends in most areas of importance to the multiple Criteria requirements and the accomplishment of the organization's mission.
481–550	8	The organization demonstrates outstanding approaches fully responsive to the multiple Criteria requirements. Approaches are fully deployed and demonstrate excellent, sustained use of measures. There is excellent integration of approaches with organizational needs. Organizational analysis, learning through innovation, and sharing of best practices are pervasive.	391–450	8	Results fully address key customer/stakeholder, market, process, and action plan requirements and include projections of future performance. Results demonstrate excellent organizational performance levels, as well as national and world leadership. Results demonstrate sustained beneficial trends in all areas of importance to the multiple Criteria requirements and the accomplishment of the organization's mission.

* "Industry" refers to other organizations performing substantially the same functions, thereby facilitating direct comparisons.

Depending upon the size of the organization and its complexity, the site visit may range from three to five days on-site. If the applicant has multiple locations, travel teams of a pair of examiners will typically go to key sites. If the applicant has multiple shifts, it can expect that examiners will conduct "walk-around questions" on each shift to verify the deployment of key approaches and the effectiveness of communication. During the site visit, the examiners may not provide any feedback to the applicant. This can be very frustrating to the organization that would like to know how the site visit is going. However, the judges and not the examiners make the final determination of which organizations are recommended to the Secretary of Commerce for the Baldrige Award.

Every evening, the examiners return to their hotel and work in their conference room sharing their observations from the day, reviewing any documentation that has been requested, updating their SVI worksheets with findings, and revising comments, as appropriate. At the conclusion of the time spent at the applicant's site, the examiners return to their hotel and spend either a day or a day and a half completing the revision of the comments, reviewing them as a team, coming to consensus about the feedback, and rescoring each item. The SVI worksheets provide the important rationale for the judges to understand why comments and scores may have changed from the consensus scorebook to the site visit scorebook.

The Evaluation and Recommendation Process—from the Judges' Perspective

The 12-member panel of judges meets twice during the award process review cycle. Following the completion of consensus, the judges convene to identify which applications will move forward to a site visit. This process is very interesting because the decisions are made solely by looking at the statistical analysis and profile of a team's scoring for each applicant. When the judges establish their cutoff point (the total number of points at which an applicant will receive a site visit), they do not yet know the identity of the organizations or the identities of the examiners. This ensures that there is no bias in the process.

Once the applicants moving on to receive a site visit have been determined—at this point by application number only—the NIST staff shares the identities of the organizations so that the judges can determine if they have any conflicts of interest that will require them to recuse themselves during the deliberation over a specific applicant.

If an applicant is not selected to move forward, the examiner team makes final revisions to the feedback report and sends it to NIST for a technical and grammar edit. For applicants that will be moving forward, NIST notifies the applicant and the examiner team to begin planning.

Following the site visits, the judges meet again. Each application is assigned a lead and a back-up judge. These judges review their assigned application, its consensus report, each SVI worksheet (there are typically 60 to 80 per applicant), and the site visit report. Every judge is also expected to read each site visit report in addition to the ones assigned as lead or backup judge. At this meeting, the lead judge presents an overview of the assigned application to the other judges. As a group, the judges identify any areas that they would like to explore with the team leader. Questions are developed, and the team leader is called. At the conclusion of the call (or possibly a second call), the judges agree that they have sufficient information to make a decision.

The applicants are reviewed by sector, and determinations of whether to recommend any for the Baldrige Award are made. Once this process has been completed for each sector and for each applicant that received a site visit, the judges take one last time to ask whether any judge would like to "revisit" an applicant that had not previously been identified as one to recommend for the award. The panel of judges may also recommend organizations not for the highest award but for having one or more categories that demonstrate best practices. All applicants receive a feedback report.

At the conclusion of the judges' meeting (typically on a Friday morning), the director of NIST conveys the recommendations to the Secretary of Commerce, and they jointly determine whether the recommended organizations would serve as appropriate role models and should receive the Baldrige Award. NIST also conducts background checks of site-visited applicants to ensure there have been no significant issues of a legal, ethical, and regulatory nature.

Generally on Monday or Tuesday of the following week, the BPEP director calls the organizations that are not recommended for the award, thanks them for their participation in the process, and encourages them to continue the journey. The Secretary of Commerce calls the highest senior leaders of the organizations that will be receiving the Baldrige Award and personally congratulates them on their achievement.

The Award Notification Process—from the Award Recipient's Perspective

The highest ranking officials of site-visited applicants are given a date and a time window of when they might expect a call from the Secretary of Commerce. You can imagine how their anxiety mounts as the clock ticks on. Rulon Stacy, former CEO of Poudre Valley Health System (a 2008 Baldrige Award recipient), described it this way, "They gave you a window when the Secretary may call . . . and as the time passed, it became more and more likely that it would be Harry Hertz [the then-director of the Baldrige Program] on the other end and not the Secretary. So, the first three times [we received Baldrige site visits], we were on pins and needles as we waited. But . . . as the hours went by, we realized what was happening, and there was disappointment. Interestingly enough, by the fourth Baldrige site visit, I had forgotten when the call was going to happen. We had become so fixated as an organization on when we would get the feedback report that we had literally forgotten when the Secretary might call. We all had to remind ourselves as we got closer to the day. The call itself was exciting, but the great excitement was to tell the entire organization. You can still see the excitement from the organization on the YouTube clip of our press conference." The YouTube video is available at https://www.youtube.com /watch?v=i_Bey0iURtU.

Scott McIntyre, managing director, PricewaterhouseCoopers Public Sector Practice (a 2014 Baldrige Award recipient), said, "Receiving a call from the Secretary of Commerce was a really exciting milestone in our quality journey underscoring not just an accomplishment for PwC, but also an obligation to continue pursuing quality improvement to uphold Baldrige's trust in our organization as an exemplar."

Ken Schiller, cofounder and co-owner of K&N Management, is a slow-talking, generally imperturbable Texan. He describes his response to learning that they had won the Baldrige Award. "It was getting late in the morning, and I was growing concerned because we had not yet received a call. We took this to be a bad sign. When the call finally did come, I felt sheer exhilaration and excitement that I will never forget. After receiving the news, I immediately walked down the hall of our corporate office blowing an air horn to announce that we had won."

David Tilton, CEO of AtlantiCare, shared his funny story. He answered the phone on a Friday afternoon seeing that it was a Washington, D.C., area code. "I answered with my standard greeting to a call, 'Hi, this is David Tilton, Administration. How can I help you?'" He said, "I thought this was another test to see if we really did things like we said we did."

Matt Fleming, president of MidwayUSA (a two-time Baldrige Award recipient), describes the time preceding the call. "The 'call' is an exciting event. Following our 2015

Baldrige site visit, we were told a call would be coming on Thursday, November 12, between 1:00 and 5:00 p.m. What we didn't know exactly was who the call would come from. If the call was from the Secretary of Commerce, it meant good news. If the call was from the director of the Baldrige Program, it meant disappointment. We had it all worked out in our heads. The Baldrige folks had a meeting scheduled with the Secretary of Commerce at 1:00. After an exchange of pleasantries, they would go over the award recipients. By 1:15, they would start making phone calls. And by 1:30, we would have our call. After 1:30, we started getting anxious, and by 2:00 we were downright nervous. We felt the longer we waited, the less likely we were to get the call we wanted. There was a small audience gathered in my office waiting with me. Even though we tried to keep ourselves busy working and talking, it was hard to focus on anything but the call. At 2:21, we were startled when the phone rang. I answered, and the welcome voice on the other end introduced herself as the Secretary of Commerce. It was the call we'd been waiting and hoping for, and the mood in the room immediately changed to extreme excitement. An enormous amount of work goes into aligning your company with the Baldrige framework and applying for the award. It's a monumental team effort. 'The call' is when the realization of all that effort and teamwork culminates, and it was one of the proudest moments of my career."

Gerry Agnes, CEO of Elevations Credit Union, a 2014 Baldrige Award recipient, describes his "call" experience. "The call time was arranged by the NIST staff to occur during a two-hour window on November 10, 2014. After about 45 minutes had passed, I really began to doubt that we'd receive the award, as I had calculated that each call to an award recipient would take about five to seven minutes, and that historically there have been two to four recipients. Doing the math, it seemed well past the time to receive a call for an award recipient. About five minutes later, my cell phone rang with an area code telephone number from 202. My heart raced, and I picked up the line and introduced myself, 'Hello, this is Gerry Agnes, how may I help you?' The person on the other end of the call said through a speakerphone, 'Well, hello, Gerry, this is Secretary Penny Pritzker.' I was so thrilled and stunned to hear her voice, as I knew that the U.S. Secretary of Commerce would not be calling an organization that would not be receiving the award. Consequently, due to my excitement and elevated adrenaline, I did not remember much of the call. Fortunately, about 10 days later we participated in a conference call with the NIST staff, the recipients, and Bob Fangmeyer, the Baldrige Program director. Unknowingly to me, Bob had been on the call with Secretary Pritzker and me. He recounted the content of the call for me. I was so delighted to relive that moment, which will now be forever engraved in my mind through Bob's retelling the story."

Tommy Gonzalez, former city manager of the City of Irving (a 2012 Baldrige Award recipient), reminisced about waiting for "the call." "First, what you are told is if the executive director of the Baldrige Program calls you, it is not good news. Then you're told, 'if the Secretary of Commerce calls you, it's good news.' So, anticipation is the first word that comes to mind when I think about that day." He continued, "Upon receiving the call, a calm came over me. My first thought was the people that make up our organization. I felt we had been a proving ground. All of us demonstrated that a municipality can indeed perform at a high level; just like any other organization in the private sector. My thoughts then went to my wife and kids who sacrificed so much over the years to make sure I made time for this effort. Finally, I thought how much time our employees committed to this effort and the impact that had on their families as well."

APPENDIX

D

Award-Winning Organizations Featured in This Book

Descriptions of these recipients are based on information in the Recipient Profiles that was current at the time the organization was named a Baldrige Award winner. If the organization has received the award twice, the description is based on information that was current at the time of the most recent award.

Manufacturing Recipient

Boeing Mobility (formerly Airlift and Tanker) (1998) designs, develops, and produces the C-17 Globemaster 111 airlifter, which is capable of carrying a 170,000-pound load. These aircraft are used by the U.S. Air Force, the company's primary customer, to transport large, heavy cargo to sites around the world. The company is headquartered in Long Beach, California, with other sites in Georgia, Missouri, and Washington, and had more than 8,700 employees. In 1997, sales exceeded $2 billion.

Service Recipients

Boeing Support Systems (formerly Aerospace Support) (2003) provides products and services, including aircraft maintenance, modification, and repair, and training for aircrews and maintenance staff to reduce life-cycle costs and increase the effectiveness of aircraft. In 2003, 97 percent of its business came from military customers. Its workforce of more than 13,000 employees were based at nine major sites in the United States and one in Australia and scattered across more than 129 secondary and smaller sites. The company's sales exceeded $4 billion.

PricewaterhouseCoopers Public Sector Practice (PwC PSP) (2014) was formed in 2005 and is one of 17 business units of PwC. Key customers are the U.S. federal government and state and local governments. It is the only group within PwC to serve this market. PwC PSP provides business advisory services, including risk consulting, management consulting, and technology consulting. Headquartered in McLean, Virginia, the firm employs nearly 1,100 people and reported a gross revenue of $265.5 million for fiscal year 2014.

Education Recipients

Kenneth W. Monfort College of Business (2004) is a college within the University of Northern Colorado located in Greeley. It was an undergraduate-only program accredited by AACSB International in both business administration and accounting—one of only five undergraduate programs in the United States to hold both accreditations. The college had 34 full-time faculty, 13 part-time adjunct faculty, and 8 administrative staff supporting a program that graduated approximately 300 students per year.

Pewaukee School District (2013) is the smallest K–12 educational system in Waukesha County, Wisconsin (outside of Milwaukee), and had an enrollment of 2,760 students in 2012. The school district includes two elementary schools, one middle school, and one high school housed on one campus. The district was staffed by 296 employees and operated under a budget of $28.6 million.

Health Care Recipients

Charleston Area Medical Center Health System (2015) includes four hospitals, the CAMC Foundation, the CAMC Health and Education Research Institute, several centers for specific treatments, and physician clinics. It boasts West Virginia's only kidney transplant center. CAMHS operates with a revenue of $956 million and a workforce of just under 7,000 employees (including nearly 800 physicians) and more than 300 volunteers.

Hill Country Memorial (2014) is an 86-bed community, nonprofit hospital that offers both general and acute care services to 10 counties in the heart of the Texas Hill Country. It provides inpatient (surgical services, including total joint replacements, and general medical), outpatient (primary care, laboratory, imaging, home health, and hospice), and emergency services. The main campus is located in Fredericksburg, Texas, and an ambulatory surgical center is located in Marble Falls, Texas, approximately 53 miles away. The workforce consists of more than 800 employees, medical staff, and volunteers. In 2013, the organization had an operating budget just under $200 million.

North Mississippi Health Services (2006, 2012) is a nonprofit, community-owned, integrated health care delivery system serving 24 rural counties in northeast Mississippi and northwest Alabama. Its six hospitals, four nursing homes, and 34 clinics provide preventive and wellness services, hospital-based emergency and acute care services, post-acute care services, and a preferred-provider organization. The workforce of 6,226 employees and 491 physicians helped the organization generate a net revenue of $730 million in 2011.

Poudre Valley Health System (2008) (now University of Colorado Health System), at the time of the award, was a locally owned and private, not-for-profit health organization serving residents of northern Colorado, Nebraska, and Wyoming in a service area covering 50,000 square miles. It offered a full spectrum of health care services including emergency/urgent, intensive, medical/surgical, maternal/child, oncology, and pediatric care. Its workforce included 4,200 staff, 550 credentialed physicians, and 800 volunteers.

Southcentral Foundation (2011) is a nonprofit health care organization established in 1982 to improve the health and social conditions of Alaska Native and American Indian people, enhance culture, and empower individuals and families to take charge of their lives. The organization provides a wide range of programs for about 55,000 Alaska Native and American Indian people. Of these, 45,000 reside in the Anchorage area, and the remaining 10,000 live in 55 remote villages accessible only by plane. The total coverage area spans some 100,000 square miles. The organization had 1,487 employees and reported $201.3 million in revenue in 2010.

SSM Health Care (2002) was the first health care recipient of the Baldrige Award. It is a private, not-for-profit health care system based in St. Louis, Missouri, that provides primary, secondary, and tertiary health care services. The system owned, managed, and was affiliated with 21 acute care hospitals and three nursing homes in Illinois, Missouri, Oklahoma, and Wisconsin. The organization had nearly 5,000 physician partners and 23,000 employees at the time of the award and had operating revenues of approximately $1.7 billion.

Small Business Recipients

K&N Management (2010) is the licensed Austin, Texas–area developer for Rudy's "Country Store" & Bar-B-Que and the creator of Mighty Fine Burgers, Fries and Shakes, two fast-casual restaurant concepts. Both feature walk-up counter service and a limited menu. The company's more than 450 employees, referred to as "team members," helped the company generate approximately $50 million in 2009.

MESA Products, Inc. (2006, 2012) is a small, privately held business headquartered in Tulsa, Oklahoma, that designs, manufactures, and installs cathodic protection systems that control the corrosion of metal surfaces in underground and submerged structures, such as pipelines and tanks. MESA sells products and materials nationwide with technical and installation services provided regionally. MESA's 139 employees helped the organization achieve $45 million in revenue in 2011.

MidwayUSA (2009, 2015) is a family-owned catalog and Internet retailer offering "Just About Everything^{SM}" for shooters, reloaders, gunsmiths, and hunters. This world leader in its market sector had more than 350 employees at the time of its second award, when it also had gross sales in excess of $350 million. Since 2004, MidwayUSA has sustained a 21.3 percent average annual growth rate in gross sales.

Park Place Lexus (2005) had two locations—Plano and Grapevine, Texas—where they sell and service new and pre-owned Lexus vehicles and sell Lexus parts to the wholesale and retail market. Their 363 members (employees) generated $387 million in revenue in 2005. Between 2000 and 2004, the company's gross profit grew by 51.3 percent. Park Place Lexus still ranks among the country's top Lexus dealers across multiple measures of performance.

PRO-TEC Coating Company (2007) was established in 1990 as a joint venture between United States Steel Corporation and Kobe Steel Ltd. of Japan. The company provides coated sheet steel primarily to the U.S. automotive industry for use in manufacturing cars, trucks, and sport utility vehicles. In

2007, its 231 associates (employees) worked 24/7 in a state-of-the-art 730,000 square-foot facility surrounded by corn and soybean fields in the small rural town of Leipsic, Ohio. Sales reached $846 million in 2006.

Stoner, Inc. (2003) is a small, family-owned business located in Lancaster County, Pennsylvania. The company's product line includes more than 300 specialized cleaners, lubricants, coatings, and car care products. At the time of the award, Stoner was the largest supplier for the United States of aerosol and bulk release agents for plastics and other molded materials. Also at the time, the company was the smallest business to receive the award with 43 full- and 5 part-time employees. From the early 1990s until 2003, Stoner increased its sales 400 percent.

Studer Group (2010) is a private, for-profit health care consulting firm providing coaching, teaching, and evidence-based tools and tactics to health care organizations and rural hospitals throughout the United States. It defines its own success based on the partner organizations it coaches, particularly how patients perceive the quality of care they receive from these organizations. Studer Group partners achieved a two to three times greater improvement during the same time period than the national average. In 2010, the 119 consultants (employees) generated revenues of approximately $47 million.

Texas Nameplate Company, Inc. (1998, 2004) became the smallest business to receive the Baldrige Award in 2004 with only 39 employees. The company is a privately held, family business that produces custom nameplates in small and frequent orders primarily for small businesses nationwide and abroad. The company increased its profitability from 36 percent to over 40 percent and, in 2003, outperformed other companies in the industry and exceeded the performance of comparable organization among *Industry Week's* 2003 benchmark companies.

Government Recipients

U.S. Army Armament Research, Development and Engineering Center (ARDEC) (2007), based in Picatinny Arsenal, New Jersey, developed 90 percent of the U.S. Army's armaments and ammunition including warheads, explosives, all sizes of firearms, battlefield sensors, and advanced weaponry based on high-power microwaves, high-energy lasers, and nanotechnology. In 2007, its annual net revenue was in excess of $1 billion. It had nearly 3,000 employees, with more than two-thirds being scientists and engineers.

Veterans Affairs Cooperative Studies Program Clinical Research Pharmacy Coordinating Center (VACSP) (2009) is a federal government organization that supports multicenter clinical trials targeting current health issues for America's veterans. The center, located in Albuquerque, New Mexico, had 112 employees providing products and services for approximately 70 clinical trials, which can last from six months to more than a decade. In 2008, the organization's productivity of $221,000 per full-time employee (FTE) compared favorably to eight top competitors, with the best competitor's performance at approximately $195,000 per FTE.

City of Irving, Texas (2012) is the thirteenth most populous city in Texas and the ninety-fourth in the United States. It is home to approximately 217,700 residents and encompasses an area of 68 square miles, including the Dallas Fort Worth International Airport. Irving's workforce included just fewer than 1,700 full-time city employees, and expanded to more than 2,000 when part-time and summer seasonal staff were included. Core services provided include law enforcement and compliance, fire protection and emergency medical, water and sewer, refuse collection, street maintenance and traffic management, parks, libraries, recreational and cultural programming, and capital improvements. It was one of five cities in the state and only 89 in the nation with a AAA rating from both Standard & Poor's (S&P) and Moody's—ratings it had maintained since 2007.

Nonprofit Recipients

Concordia Publishing House (2011) is the St. Louis, Missouri-based publishing arm of The Lutheran Church–Missouri Synod. It was founded in 1869 to provide its members with Christian ministry resources for worship, education, and nurturing of their faith. In 2011, the company provided over 8,000 products in a variety of formats and languages. It had a workforce of 247 employees and revenues of $35 million.

Elevations Credit Union (2014) is a member-owned, nonprofit credit union serving over 106,000 people through 11 branches and 323 employees in Colorado's Boulder, Broomfield, Larimer, and Adams counties. It offers a wide range of financial products and services, including checking and savings accounts, auto loans, student loans, mortgages, home equity lines of credit, business loans, credit cards, and financial planning. In 2013, Elevations Credit Union had over $1.4 billion in assets, $66 million in gross revenue, and $9.5 million in net revenue.

Mid-America Transplant Services (2015) is a private, nonprofit organ procurement organization and eye and tissue bank serving 84 counties in eastern Missouri, southern Illinois, and northeastern Arkansas. It has a workforce of 193 employees and an annual budget of $39 million.

Note: Recipient Profiles are prepared by the Baldrige Program and posted on its website, http://patapsco.nist.gov /Award_Recipients/index.cfm. In addition, award application summaries from these organizations and other award recipients can be found on this same web page.

Recipients of the Top Level Award in Baldrige-Based State Programs

Mary Greeley Medical Center (2014—Iowa Recognition for Performance Excellence) is a publicly owned, 220-bed hospital located in Ames, Iowa. Main health care services offered include general and acute inpatient care, ambulatory surgery, emergency services, home health services, and hospice care. A medical staff of over 200 providers covering 35 specialties and subspecialties together with 1,286 staff deliver services in a professional and compassionate manner.

Methodist Health System (2015—Texas Award for Performance Excellence) delivers its health care services through four hospitals in the north Texas area with inpatient, outpatient, and emergency care. Its main health care service offerings are trauma, transplant, neurosurgery, surgery, general medicine, cardiology, and obstetrics. MHS has more than 7,000 active employees, 1,127 volunteers, and 390 students. It has a net revenue of over $1 million.

Recipients of the Gold and Silver Awards in the AHCA/NCAL Quality Award, the Baldrige-Based Program for the Long-Term Care Industry

Kindred Nursing and Rehabilitation—Mountain Valley (Gold 2011) is a 68-bed facility located in rural Kellogg, Idaho, that provides long-term care and short-term rehabilitation. It has a staff of 90 employees.

Maine Veterans' Home—Caribou (Silver 2016) has a 40-bed long-term care/skilled nursing unit and a 30-bed early dementia assisted living unit. It is located in the most northeastern town in the continental United States in a very rural area.

Maine Veterans' Home—Machias (Silver 2015) is a 30-bed secured assisted living facility (ALF) that specializes in memory impairment care and resides on the campus of Down East Community Hospital (DECH) located in rural Washington County, Machias, Maine.

Maine Veterans' Home—Scarborough (Gold 2016) is a 120-bed, dually certified skilled nursing facility with an attached 30-bed assisted living facility (ALF). It is located just outside of Portland.

Afterword

The goal of improving organizational performance, particularly in health care, has been a central focus of the work of Glenn Bodinson and Kay Kendall. They not only make the case for why programs such as those based on the Baldrige Excellence Framework are necessary, but also explore the frustrations and accomplishments of leaders who have been successful in making the journey to world-class quality performance. In this incredibly insightful book, they have garnered the common principles and strategies that successful corporate leaders spanning many different industries have in common.

Peter Drucker is often credited with the observation "Culture eats strategy for lunch." Nowhere is this observation more prescient than in the quest to focus and align the organization to the pursuit of excellence, in engaging each member of the team to be committed to this purpose.

Having worked with Glenn and Kay, I can provide testimony that this process is not easy. In fact, our organization has had many fits and starts. However, when we look at our Quality Dashboard now, the dials are all moving in the right direction! Within the context of the AHCA's Quality Award Program, 27 of our 30 facilities have achieved Bronze Recognition, and we have been recognized with our first Silver Awards. This simply would not have happened without Glenn and Kay's sage advice, coaching, and support. I hope that this book will inspire you to embark on your own journey to performance excellence.

Fred Benjamin, FACHE
Chief Operating Officer
Medicalodges, Inc.

Notes

Chapter 1

1. The Malcolm Baldrige National Quality Improvement Act of 1987, Public Law 100-107, http://www.nist.gov/baldrige/about/improvement_act.cfm.
2. Baldrige Performance Excellence Program, *2015–2016 Baldrige Excellence Framework: A Systems Approach to Improving Your Organization's Performance* (Gaithersburg, MD: U.S. Department of Commerce, National Institute of Standards and Technology, 2015), 44. http://www.nist.gov/baldrige.
3. Albert N. Link and John T. Scott, *Economic Evaluation of the Baldrige Performance Excellence Program*, December 2011, http://www.nist.gov/baldrige/publications/economic_evaluation_2011.cfm.
4. John R. Griffith, "Understanding High-Reliability Organizations: Are Baldrige Recipients Models?" *The Journal of Healthcare Management* 60, no. 1 (Jan/Feb 2015): 44. http://www.creative-healthcare.com/pdf/Hi-Reliability-Organizations-Are-Baldrige-Recipients-Models.pdf.
5. Brian Cazzell and Jeffrey M. Ulmer, "Measuring Excellence: A Closer Look at Malcolm Baldrige National Quality Award Winners in the Manufacturing Category," *The Journal of Management & Innovation* 4, no. 1 (2009): 136.
6. Baldrige Performance Excellence Program, *2015–2016 Baldrige Excellence Framework: A Systems Approach to Improving Your Organization's Performance* (Gaithersburg, MD: U.S. Department of Commerce, National Institute of Standards and Technology, 2015), 39. http://www.nist.gov/baldrige.

Chapter 2

1. Baldrige Performance Excellence Program, *2015–2016 Baldrige Excellence Framework: A Systems Approach to Improving Your Organization's*

Performance (Gaithersburg, MD: U.S. Department of Commerce, National Institute of Standards and Technology, 2015), 54, http://www.nist.gov/baldrige.

2. Harvard Business Review Analytic Services, "The Impact of Employee Engagement on Performance," 2013, 1, https://hbr.org/resources/pdfs/comm/achievers/hbr_achievers_report_sep13.pdf.

3. Robyn Reilly, "Five Ways to Improve Employee Engagement Now." *Gallup Business Journal*, January 7, 2014, 1, http://www.gallup.com/businessjournal/166667/five-ways-improve-employee-engagement.aspx.

4. Robyn Reilly, "Five Ways to Improve Employee Engagement Now," *Gallup Business Journal*, January 7, 2014, 2–3, http://www.gallup.com/businessjournal/166667/five-ways-improve-employee-engagement.aspx.

5. "People Practices and the Bottom Line," Boston Consulting Group Perspectives, accessed March 20, 2016, https://www.bcgperspectives.com/content/articles/people_management_human_resources_leadership_from_capability_to_profitability/?chapter=2.

6. Karlyn Borysenko, "What Was Management Thinking? The High Cost of Employee Turnover," April 22, 2015, http://www.eremedia.com/tlnt/what-was-leadership-thinking-the-shockingly-high-cost-of-employee-turnover/.

7. Emma Seppala and Kim Cameron, "Proof That Positive Work Cultures Are More Productive," *Harvard Business Review*, December 1, 2015, https://hbr.org/2015/12/proof-that-positive-work-cultures-are-more-productive.

8. PwC Advisory, *An HR Perspective. 2015 Employee Engagement Landscape Study: Championing Greatness or Capturing Mediocrity*, November 2015, 2.

9. PwC Advisory, *An HR Perspective. 2015 Employee Engagement Landscape Study: Championing Greatness or Capturing Mediocrity*, November 2015, 7.

10. James Kouzes and Barry Posner, *The Leadership Challenge* (San Francisco: Jossey-Bass, 2012), 340.

11. Jim Collins, *Good to Great* (New York: HarperCollins Publishers, Inc., 2001), 39.

12. Quint Studer, "If It Really Is a 'Soft Skill,' Then Why Is It So Hard?" (blog), April 11, 2012, https://www.studergroup.com/resources/news-media/healthcare-publications-resources/insights/april-2012/if-it-really-is-a-soft-skill-then-why-is-it-so-har.

13. Diane Berry, Lily Mok, and Thomas Otter. "CFO Advisory: Employee Engagement Impacts Financial Outcomes and

Business Risk," Gartner Executive Programs G00249694, March 13, 2013, 1, https://www.gartner.com/doc/2369417/cfo-advisory -employee-engagement-impacts.

Chapter 3

1. Kevin Freiberg and Jackie Freiberg, *Nuts! Southwest Airlines' Crazy Recipe for Business and Personal Success* (Austin, TX: Bard Press, Inc., 1996), 151.
2. Dawn Marie Bailey, "Collins on Baldrige as a SMAC Recipe, Discipline, Creativity, and Paranoia," *Blogrige*, April 28, 2015, http://nistbaldrige.blogs.govdelivery.com/2015/04/28/collins-on -baldrige-as-a-smac-recipe-discipline-creativity-and-paranoia/.
3. Sister Mary Jean Ryan, FSM, *On Becoming Exceptional* (Milwaukee: American Society for Quality, Quality Press, 2007), 55–60.
4. Dawn Marie Bailey, "How Values, Quarterly Coaching Address Clinician Burnout, Improve Engagement," *Blogrige*, May 21, 2015, http://nistbaldrige.blogs.govdelivery.com/2015/05/21/how-values-quar terly-coaching-address-clinician-burnout-improve-engagement/.
5. James Kouzes and Barry Posner, *The Leadership Challenge* (San Francisco: Jossey-Bass, 2012) 133–134.
6. Michael D. Basch, *Customer Culture: How FedEx and Other Great Companies Put the Customer First Every Day* (Upper Saddle River: Prentice Hall PTR, 2002), 240.
7. Dawn Marie Bailey, "A Customer Guarantee Absolutely Dependent on Workforce Engagement," *Blogrige*, March 17, 2016, http://nist baldrige.blogs.govdelivery.com/2016/03/17/a-customer-guarantee -absolutely-dependent-on-workforce-engagement/.
8. Baldrige Performance Excellence Program, *2015–2016 Baldrige Excellence Framework: A Systems Approach to Improving Your Organization's Performance* (Gaithersburg, MD: U.S. Department of Commerce, National Institute of Standards and Technology, 2015), 7, http://www.nist.gov/baldrige.

Chapter 4

1. PwC Advisory, *An HR Perspective. 2015 Employee Engagement Landscape Study: Championing Greatness or Capturing Mediocrity*, November 2015, 11, 13. http://www.pwc.com/us/en/hr-management /publications/employee-engagement-landscape-2015.html
2. John P. Kotter, "What Leaders Really Do," *Harvard Business Review*, December 2001, 86.

3. PwC Advisory, *An HR Perspective*, 8.
4. "Lack of Trust in Leadership Is the Biggest Issue Impacting Perfor-mance—How Do You Fix the Problem?," http://tolerosolutions.com/employees-lack-trust-in-leadership-biggest-issue-impacting-performance/.
5. Stephen M. R. Covey, "How the Best Leaders Build Trust," Leader-shipNow, http://www.leadershipnow.com/CoveyOnTrust.html.

Chapter 5

1. TINYpulse, "7 Vital Trends Disrupting Today's Workplace: Results and Data from 2013 TINYpulse Employee Engagement Survey," https://www.tinypulse.com/resources/employee-engagement-survey-2013.
2. Kevin Kruse, "Transparency Eats Culture for Lunch," December 2, 2013, http://www.kevinkruse.com/transparency-eats-culture-for-lunch/.
3. Joe Folkman, "Top 9 Leadership Behaviors That Drive Employee Commitment," Zenger Folkman, 2010, http://zengerfolkman.com/wp-content/uploads/2013/05/ZFA-9-Behaviors.pdf.
4. Jim Collins, *Good to Great* (New York: HarperCollins Publishers, Inc., 2001), 74.
5. Sister Mary Jean Ryan, FSM, *On Becoming Exceptional* (Milwaukee: American Society for Quality, Quality Press, 2007), 69.
6. Jeanne Chircop, "Solid Commitment to People Is Main Ingredient for Texas Restaurant Excellence," ASQ Case Study, March 2011, 2.

Chapter 6

1. John P. Kotter. "Leading Change: Why Transformation Efforts Fail." *Harvard Business Review*, January 2007, https://hbr.org/2007/01/leading-change-why-transformation-efforts-fail, 97.

Chapter 7

1. Keith McFarland, *The Breakthrough Company: How Everyday Compa-nies Become Extraordinary Performers* (New York: Crown Business, 2008), 194–195.
2. Jim Collins, *How the Mighty Fall: and Why Some Companies Never Give In* (New York: HarperCollins Publishers Inc., 2009), 182.
3. Dawn Marie Bailey, "Insights from Leaders of 2014 Baldrige Award Recipients (Part 2)," *Blogrige*, April 23, 2015, http://nistbaldrige.blogs.govdelivery.com/2015/04/23/insights-from-leaders-of-2014-baldrige-award-recipients-part-2/.

4. Ayla Ellison, "10 Recent Hospital Bankruptcies, Closures," *Becker's Hospital Review* (blog), January 25, 2016, http://www.beckers hospitalreview.com/finance/10-recent-hospital-bankruptcies -closures-january25.html.

Chapter 9

1. Baldrige testimonials, http://www.nist.gov/baldrige/enter/testimo nials.cfm.

Chapter 10

1. Jim Collins, "Good to Great," *Fast Company*, October 2001, http:// www.fastcompany.com/43811/good-great.
2. Sister Mary Jean Ryan, *On Becoming Exceptional: SSM Health Care's Journey to Baldrige and Beyond* (Milwaukee: American Society for Quality, Quality Press, 2007), 41.
3. *Integrated Leaders Build a Culture of Trust*, Physician Leadership Institute, 2015, http://physicianleadership.org/wp-content/uploads /2016/01/Integrated-Leaders-Build-a-Culture-of-Trust.pdf.
4. E. David Spong and Debbie J. Collard, *The Making of a World Class Organization* (Milwaukee: American Society for Quality, Quality Press, 2009), xxi.
5. Ibid., xxi–xxii.

Chapter 11

1. Jim McElgunn, "How to Replace a Culture of Employee Entitlement," *PROFITguide* (blog), April 24, 2012, www.profitguide.com /manage-grow/human-resources/how-to-fight-the-business -crippling-entitlement-mindset-30385.
2. Ibid.
3. Erica Spelman, "Entitlement in the Workplace," *Zappos* (blog), August 20, 2014, http://www.zapposinsights.com/blog/item/entitlement -in-the-workplace.
4. Jessica Tyler, "Employee Engagement and Labor Relations," Gallup, September 10, 2009, www.gallup.com/businessjournal/122849 /employee-engagement-labor-relations.aspx.
5. Robert Lavigna, "Why Government Workers Are Harder to Motivate," *Harvard Business Review*, November 28, 2014.
6. Jessica Tyler, "Employee Engagement and Labor Relations." http:// www.gallup.com/businessjournal/122849/employee-engagement -labor-relations.aspx

Chapter 12

1. Quint Studer, *Straight A Leadership: Alignment, Action, Accountability* (Gulf Breeze: Firestarter Publishing, 2009), 114.
2. Jonathon Thorpe, Waheed Baqui, Dan Witters, Jim Harter, Sangeeta Agrawal, Kirti Kanitkar, and James Pappas, "Workplace Engagement and Workers' Compensation Claims as Predictors for Patient Safety Culture," *Journal of Patient Safety* 8, no. 4 (December 2012): 194–201.
3. Jeff Burger and Luke Sutton, "How Employee Engagement Can Improve a Hospital's Health," *Gallup Business Journal*, April 3, 2014, http://www.gallup.com/businessjournal/168149/employee-engage ment-improve-hospital-health.aspx.
4. Robyn Reilly, "Five Ways to Improve Employee Engagement Now," *Gallup Business Journal*, January 7, 2014, 3, http://www.gallup.com/ businessjournal/166667/five-ways-improve-employee-engagement .aspx.
5. Dawn Marie Bailey, "How Can You Apply Safety Lessons from Steel to Your Organization?," *Blogrige*, March 10, 2015, http://nist baldrige.blogs.govdelivery.com/2015/03/10/how-can-you-apply -safety-lessons-from-steel-to-your-organization/.
6. "100 Best Companies All-Stars," *Fortune* 171, no. 4 (March 15, 2015): 134.
7. Grant T. Savage, "Patient and Employee Safety: Leadership, Rework, and Workarounds" (presentation, Health Services Research Colloquium, University of Alabama at Birmingham, February 28, 2011).

Chapter 13

1. Baldrige testimonials, http://www.nist.gov/baldrige/enter/testimo nials.cfm.
2. Dawn Marie Bailey, "Why Status Quo Was Not Enough for This Role-Model Workforce," *Blogrige*, March 24, 2016, http://nist baldrige.blogs.govdelivery.com/2016/03/24/why-status-quo-was -not-enough-for-this-role-model-workforce/.
3. Dawn Marie Bailey, "Collins on Baldrige as a SMAC Recipe, Discipline, Creativity, and Paranoia," *Blogrige*, April 28, 2015, http:// nistbaldrige.blogs.govdelivery.com/2015/04/28/collins-on -baldrige-as-a-smac-recipe-discipline-creativity-and-paranoia/.
4. James Kouzes and Barry Posner, *The Leadership Challenge* (San Francisco: Jossey-Bass, 2012), 16–17.

5. Christine Schaefer, "With Humility and Hard Work, Elevations Credit Union Keeps Climbing Higher," *Blogrige*, March 23, 2014, http://nistbaldrige.blogs.govdelivery.com/2016/03/23/with -humility-and-hard-work-elevations-credit-union-keeps-climbing -higher/.

Chapter 14

1. Leigh Buchanan, "We Will be the Best-Run Business in America," *Inc.*, January 24, 2012.

Chapter 16

1. Dawn Marie Bailey, "One of the Most Powerful in Health Care," *Blogrige*, September 20, 2012, http://nistbaldrige.blogs.govdelivery .com/2012/09/20/one-of-the-most-powerful-in-health-care/.
2. Joe Folkman, "Top 9 Leadership Behaviors That Drive Employee Commitment," Zenger Folkman, 2010, http://zengerfolkman.com/ white-papers/
3. Sister Mary Jean Ryan, *On Becoming Exceptional: SSM Health Care's Journey to Baldrige and Beyond* (Milwaukee: Quality Press, 2007), 25.

Appendix C

1. David T. Kearns and David A. Nadler, *Prophets in the Dark: How Xerox Reinvented Itself and Beat Back the Japanese* (New York City: Harper-Business, 1992), 247.

Index

About the Authors

Kay Kendall is the CEO and principal of BaldrigeCoach. She spent more than 20 years as a quality executive leading large-scale change initiatives across diverse industries—aerospace, semiconductor automation equipment, computers and storage devices, and pharmaceuticals. She completed a five-year assignment as a Lean Six Sigma Master Black Belt in 2009 when she joined BaldrigeCoach. She also has extensive experience implementing the Balanced Scorecard, Hoshin Kanri, and benchmarking to deliver results. She currently works with organizations, coaching them on their journey toward Performance Excellence.

From 2002 through 2005, Kay served on the Panel of Judges for the Malcolm Baldrige National Quality Program after serving as an Examiner and Senior Examiner for the program for six years. She continues to serve as an Alumni for the program. Kay served four years as a Master Examiner and Team Leader for the AHCA/NCAL Quality Award Program. She served as a Judge for the California Award for Performance Excellence for five years and for the Robert W. Carey Award for seven years, and is in her fifth year as a Judge for Partners in Performance Excellence, the Baldrige-based regional program serving New York, Massachusetts, Connecticut, and Rhode Island. Kay has facilitated examiner training for the Baldrige program since 1998, as well as for other Baldrige-based programs. Kay also served five years as a Director-at-Large for the Alliance.

Kay is frequently invited to speak at international conferences on a variety of topics, including change leadership. She also has facilitated workshops with audiences in the several hundreds and has guided organizations in their strategic planning processes.

Glenn Bodinson, FACHE, founded BaldrigeCoach in 1989 to help organizations become more productive, profitable, and fun places to work by harnessing the power of performance excellence. Glenn is on the Advisory Board of the Methodist Dallas Hospital and a member of the Methodist Health System Corporate Quality Committee. BaldrigeCoach helped Methodist Health System win the Texas Award for Performance Excellence in 2015, the highest level award given by the program.

Glenn served as the Vice President of the Hogan Center for Performance Excellence where he developed and delivered the curricula for its two-year transformation program. Graduates of this program include Baldrige recipients Branch Smith Printing, Park Place Lexus, Karlee, Texas Nameplate, and Marlow Industries.

Glenn's experience includes service as a Malcolm Baldrige National Quality Award Examiner in 1992, 1993, 2012, 2013, and 2014, and Senior Examiner and Team Leader in 2015 and an Alumni in 2016. He served as a Texas Quality Award Judge from 1994 to 1999, and as a Shingo Prize Examiner from 2000 to 2015 and Team Leader in 2016. He served six years as a Judge for the Robert W. Carey Award Program and served five years as a Master Examiner and Team Leader for the AHCA/NCAL National Quality Award. He also is serving his fifth year as a National Director on the Board of The Alliance, the consortium of Baldrige-based State and local programs.

Glenn is a Fellow of the American College of Healthcare Executives (FACHE) and a Fellow of the American Society for Quality (ASQ). He is a Certified Six Sigma Black Belt (CSSBB).

Kay and Glenn's first book, *The Executive Guide to Understanding and Implementing Baldrige in Healthcare: Evidence-Based Excellence®* is available at Amazon.com.

BaldrigeCoach When organizations are facing challenges to sustainability or opportunities for unprecedented growth, their leaders look for knowledgeable resources to help navigate through the uncharted course. BaldrigeCoach has become the trusted advisors to CEOs by accelerating excellence and transforming organizations through customized assessments and solutions that help organizations become more productive and efficient while delighting customers and achieving high levels of results across multiple measures of performance. Our proven record includes 18 clients who are recipients of the Malcolm Baldrige National Quality Award, 36 clients who have received their top-level State Quality Awards, and 12 clients who have been recognized with the AHCA/NCAL Gold Quality Award.

We enjoy connecting with our readers online. Below are the places you can find us. Make sure to mention that you read our book, *Leading the Malcolm Baldrige Way: How World-Class Leaders Align Their Organizations to Achieve Exceptional Results.*

Website
www.baldrigecoach.com
www.baldrigebooks.com
www.bronze-to-silver.com
www.silver-to-gold.com

LinkedIn
www.linkedin.com/in/kaykendallbaldrigecoach
www.linkedin.com/in/glennbodinson
www.linkedin.com/company/baldrigecoach-inc-

Twitter
www.twitter.com/kayakendall

Book us for your next event!
We are highly rated speakers, sought after coaches, and trusted advisors to senior leaders. Contact us at:

Glenn@Baldrige-Coach.com
972-489-5430

Kay@Baldrige-Coach.com
972-489-3611